CARLO GESUALDO

PRINCE OF VENOSA

MUSICIAN AND MURDERER

PLATE I

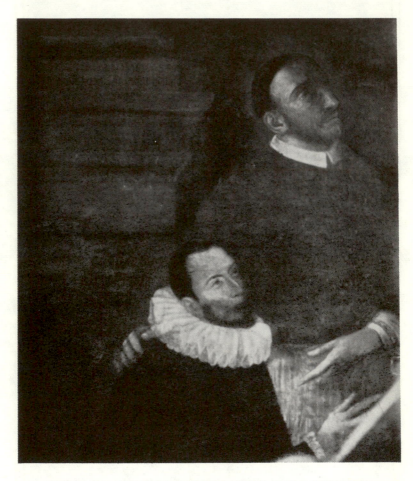

DON CARLO GESUALDO WITH HIS UNCLE, CARLO BORROMEO

CARLO GESUALDO

PRINCE OF VENOSA

MUSICIAN AND MURDERER

BY

CECIL GRAY AND PHILIP HESELTINE

With 34 Musical Examples in
the text and 8 full-page plates

GREENWOOD PRESS, PUBLISHERS
WESTPORT, CONNECTICUT

Originally published in 1926
by Kegan Paul, Trench, Trubner & Co., Ltd., London

First Greenwood Reprinting 1971

Library of Congress Catalogue Card Number 76-104268

SBN 8371-3934-1

Printed in the United States of America

To

SIGNOR SALVATORE DI GIACOMO

Poet, Historian, and Scholar,
this study of his compatriot
is respectfully dedicated by
the grateful Authors, as an
inadequate return for his
invaluable assistance.

CONTENTS

LIST OF ILLUSTRATIONS.

MUSICAL EXAMPLES

IN THE TEXT

IN THE APPENDIX

GESUALDO

[N.B.—In these musical examples, the note-values of the original are generally halved (i.e. ♩ = ♪ of the original) and bar-lines have been inserted, accidentals remaining in force throughout the bar in the modern fashion. None of the examples have been transposed out of their original keys.]

PREFACE

The present writers are by no means the first to occupy themselves with Carlo Gesualdo, Prince of Venosa. The main difference between them and their predecessors, however, is that those of the latter who have been interested in his work have almost entirely neglected his biography, while those who have occupied themselves with the dramatic incidents of his life have for the most part been entirely unaware of his great artistic significance. Consequently, the authors feel that they can reasonably claim the present effort to be the only tolerably complete study of Carlo Gesualdo, as both man and musician, that has yet appeared. This is not to say that they regard it as being in any sense final or definitive. Though no effort has been spared to make it complete, it is more than probable that future investigators will be able to discover fresh material, particularly on the biographical side. That they have been able to do as much as they have is almost entirely due to the extraordinary kindness, courtesy, and disinterested enthusiasm of Sig. Salvatore di Giacomo, who is one of the greatest living authorities on Neapolitan history and art. It might be too much to say that without his help and sympathy this little book would never have been written; but it would certainly be much more imperfect and incomplete than it actually is. Their thanks are also due to Messrs. Boris Chroustchoff,

PREFACE

Norman Douglas and Sacheverell Sitwell, for valuable help and suggestions; to Miss Gladys Field, Miss Beatrice Hughes-Pope and Messrs. Albert Whitehead, Taylor Harris and Joseph Maclean, for singing through several of the madrigals of Gesualdo, thus affording the writers a more precise idea of the music than could possibly be attained through a mere study of it on paper; to the Director of the Uffizi Gallery in Florence for permission to reproduce the picture of the Palazzo Sansevero prior to the earthquake of 1688; and also to the Sindaco of Gesualdo for his assistance in procuring a photograph of the painting in the church of the Convento dei Cappuccini.

CECIL GRAY
PHILIP HESELTINE

PART I.

Life of Carlo Gesualdo

PART I

The Life of Carlo Gesualdo

Gesualdo, the Prince of Venosa,
Was a truly astounding composer.
Though much of his history
Is shrouded in mystery,
We have here all the facts we DO *know, Sir!*

His most Illustrious and Serene Highness Don
Carlo, third Prince of Venosa, eighth Count of Consa,
fifteenth Lord of Gesualdo, Marquis of Laino,
Rotondo and S. Stefano, Duke of Caggiano, Lord of
Frigento, Acquaputida, Paterno, S. Manco, Boneto,
Luceria, S. Lupolo, etc., was descended from one of
the oldest and noblest families in the kingdom of the
Two Sicilies. The first mention of the name of
Gesualdo in Neapolitan history dates back to the dark
ages which intervene between the fall of Rome and
the establishment of the mediæval Empire by Charle-
magne, and to the time of the ancient kingdom of the
Lombards. During the siege of Benevento by
Constans II, Emperor of Byzantium, Duke Romualdo,
who was in command of the city, finding himself
hard pressed, resolved to send his trusty servant
Gesualdo to his father Grimoaldo, King of Lombardy,
for assistance. Gesualdo accomplished the first part
of his task successfully, and a large army was got

together by the king in order to march to the assistance
of his son.   In the meanwhile, Gesualdo was sent
back to announce the approach of reinforcements,
but had the misfortune to fall into the hands of the
besiegers. Thereupon the Greek Emperor suggested to
his prisoner that he should go up underneath the walls
of the beleaguered city and declare to the Duke his
master that he had been unable to obtain reinforcements, and that the only course left open was to
surrender the city.   For this act of treachery, great
rewards were promised him.   Seeming to comply with
the suggestion, Gesualdo was led out by his captors
to within hailing distance of the walls, but instead of
delivering the false message as he had agreed to do,
he spoke to the Duke as follows :—" My lord, take
heart, because this night the valiant Grimoaldo, your
father, together with the flower of his troops, is
encamped upon the banks of the river Sangro, and
will speedily fall upon these barbarous invaders who
will be forced to take refuge in flight if they are to
escape the sharp points of the avenging Lombard
spears.   Wherefore I beseech you that my wife and
children be commended to your care and protection,
because this ruffianly crew, finding themselves to be
deceived by me in not giving you false information,
will without doubt slay me."

In this, Gesualdo guessed aright.   His head was
cut off and fired by a catapult into the city where it
was taken to the Duke, who with great respect kissed
it, and set upon it his ducal crown.   And this, according to some, was the reason for the presence of a ducal
crown on the family coat of arms, and the origin of the
illustrious house which ever afterwards claimed as

their ancestor this Gesualdo " who for this glorious act of devotion deserves to be numbered among the noblest heroes renowned in story."

The chronicles go on to say that after this vile and barbarous act, Constans precipitately raised the siege and retired on Naples. A body of Lombards, under the command of Count Capo Mitola, burning with righteous zeal to revenge the death of Gesualdo, and to punish the perfidious Greek, caught up with and attacked the Imperial rear-guard and cut it to pieces, none thereof escaping. And this, according to the testimony of Paulus Diaconus, took place near the river Calore.

Although this Gesualdo has generally been considered to be the founder of the noble family which bears his name, he does not seem to be a direct ancestor, at least in the male line, for in subsequent chronicles one reads of a Guglielmo (William) lord of Gesualdo and son of Roger Duke of Puglia, who was the illegitimate son of the great Robert Guiscard, the Norman conqueror of Southern Italy in the 11th century. This origin of the family is confirmed by inscriptions on buildings and tombstones dedicated to its members. On the other hand, it is quite probable that the title and estate of Gesualdo came to this Guglielmo through his marriage with a female heiress of the earlier Lombard dynasty.

From this time onward, the name of Gesualdo occurs frequently in the pages of Neapolitan history. The son of Guglielmo, named Elia, took the side of the Pope in the great struggle of Manfred with the Church, and was consequently deprived of his honours by the king and banished from Naples. On

Manfred's downfall he was reinstated. His son
Niccolo was a great warrior and captain of the City of
Naples and its district; another Elia was Grand Con-
stable and Marshal of the kingdom in 1183; another
Niccolo was Captain General and Justiciary of the
Basilicata and Regent of the Vicaria in 1290; and
Ruggiero was Marshal of the kingdom and Justiciary
of Otranto 1385. We also read that Ladislaus, the
first king of Naples belonging to the house of Aragon
(c. 1400), a great lover of jousting, was thrown to
earth by a Gesualdo of Gesualdo, " a youth of
monstrous strength and great skill, who in jousting
and martial feats unhorsed every adversary by the
strength of his lance and the force of his arm."

In 1494, Luigi, eleventh Lord of Gesualdo, and
third Count of Consa, took part in a rebellion against
the king, Ferrante II, and was deprived of his feudal
rights. Two years later he was forgiven and reinstated in his privileges, and promptly proceeded to
rebel again. Accordingly the king, then Federico of
Aragon, gave to his captain Gonsalvo Ferrandez de
Corduba the city of Consa together with the castles of
Sant Andria and Sant Mena, and other possessions
formerly appertaining to the house of Gesualdo.
However, this period of disgrace and eclipse did not
last long. In 1506, as the result of an agreement
arrived at by France and Spain, the house of
Gesualdo received back its lands and fortresses, and
in 1546 the principality of Venosa was added to its
territorial possessions.

The family distinguished itself in other fields as
well as on the field of battle. Ascanio was Archbishop of Bari, and Alfonso was Cardinal Archbishop

of Naples, and at one time had a good chance of being
made Pope.[1] From a dedication of a book of
madrigals by Gasparo della Porta to the afore-
mentioned Ascanio we learn that " The family of
Gesualdo has always held in esteem the art of music,
and many knights and princes who have adorned
every age, have often exchanged the pen for the
sword, and musical instruments for the pen, as witness
whereof the most excellent Prince of Venosa "—the
subject of the present study. His father, Fabrizio,
according to a contemporary writer, Ammirato (*Delle
famiglie nobili di Napoli*) was " greatly appreciative
of music, and in this noble art one finds many learned
compositions of his which are held in great esteem by
the *cognoscenti*. Moreover he maintained in his own
house an academy of all the musicians of the
city, whom he supported and favoured most
courteously." But I am inclined to think that the
writer has, to a certain extent at least, confused the
father with the son, for nowhere else does one find it
mentioned that Fabrizio was a composer. Nevertheless it is certain that he was a prince of great culture
and refinement. He had four children, two sons,
Luigi and Carlo, and two daughters, Isabella and
Vittoria.

Carlo, born about 1560 (some say 1557) was the
second son, and consequently was not heir to the
title and family estates. He seems to have evinced
early in life a remarkable aptitude for music which

---

[1] A less creditable member of the family figures in a *novella* of Bandello
(Part II., No. 7), entitled, *L'Abbate Gesualdo vuol rapir una giovane, e
resta vituperosamente da lei ferito, et ella, saltata nel fiume, s'aiuta* (The
Abbe Gesualdo, in attempting to molest a young woman, was grievously
wounded by her, while she, leaping into the river, effected her escape).

could only have been intensified and stimulated by his environment and opportunities. He is said to have been taught by Pomponio Nenna, but considering that the latter was only born in 1560 or possibly even later, this seems improbable. However that may be, he learnt composition and received instruction in the playing of several instruments. As an executant and improviser he rapidly attained to great proficiency; he was particularly renowned as a performer on the *arciliuto*, or bass-lute. In fact, his early reputation seems to be rather that of an executant than a composer, and of a musical Maecenas and art patron. A contemporary writer on music, Scipione Cerreto, in his book entitled *Della prattica Musica, vocale et Strumentale*, says of him : " Not only did this Prince take great delight in music, but also for his pleasure and entertainment did keep at his court, at his own expense, many excellent composers, players and singers; so that I do often think that if this nobleman had lived at the time of the Greeks of antiquity, when one who was ignorant of music was considered uneducated, however great his knowledge of other things (as witness whereof the story of the philosopher Themistocles who was greatly discomfited and put to shame for not being able, at a certain banquet, to play upon some instrument) they would have raised up unto his memory a statue, not of mere marble, but of purest gold."

The names of many members of this private academy, or *camerata*—strikingly similar to the more famous one of Count Bardi in Florence at the same time—are known to us. Chief among them are Scipione Stella, a composer; Giandomenico Montella, organist, harpist, and lutenist; Fabrizio Filomarino, a skilled performer on the seven-stringed guitar; Scipione Dentice, a writer on music and player of the *cembalo*, who published five books of madrigals between 1591 and 1607; Antonio Grifone, a violist; Rocco Rodio, one of the most distinguished musicians of his time, especially on the theoretical side; and Leonardo Primavera dell' Arpa, also one of the most eminent composers and executants of the period.

This *camerata* was not exclusively musical, however. Many poets used to be present at its gatherings, among them Torquato Tasso, the foremost poet of his age. He seems to have been at that time staying with Count Manso, the same whom Milton visited during his Italian travels, and to whom he addressed the Latin poem beginning

Haec quoque, Manse, tuae meditantur carmina laudi

and the Count seems also to have been a friend of Gesualdo.[1] The latter met Tasso about Easter in 1588, and a close friendship was established between them which was only terminated by the poet's death in 1595. Three of the latter's poems are addressed to Gesualdo—the sonnets, which begin with the lines "*Alta prole di regi eletta in terra*" and "*Carlo, il vostro leon c'ha nero il vello*" (an allusion to the heraldic device of the Gesualdo family, a black lion with five red lilies upon a silver field), and a *canzone* in which are celebrated his most distinguished ancestors. There is little doubt, moreover, that this

---

[1] It is interesting to note that in 1638 Milton sent home from Venice a number of books, " particularly a chest or two of choice music-books of the best masters flourishing about that time in Italy—namely Luca Marenzio, Monte Verdi, Horatio Vecchi, Cifra, *the Prince of Venosa* and several others " (*vide* W. Godwin, *Lives of Edward and John Philips*, Appendix II.).

friendship played a very important part in Gesualdo's artistic career.   In the first place Tasso was the greatest living exponent of the literary form known as the madrigal.   From 1592 onwards he sent his noble friend no less than 40, written expressly for him to set to music, eight of which are actually among the Prince's published compositions, namely, *Gelo ha Madonna il seno, Mentre Madonna, Se da si nobil mano, Felice primavera, Caro amoroso meo, Se così dolce e il duolo, Se taccio il duol s'avanza, Non e questa la mano.*   It is quite possible that others of the forty were also set to music by Gesualdo, but have not survived.   It is certainly beyond doubt that the prevailing spirit of his music, its passionate sorrow, elegiac tenderness, and eloquent despair, are essentially a musical paraphrase or reproduction of the spirit of Tasso's poetry.   Five letters from the poet to his friend have come down to us, and a free translation of them will be found in the appendix.

The young prince, together with his illustrious friend and members of the camerata, would often retire to his castle of S. Antonio in Mergellina, just outside Naples; and they would spend whole nights out in the bay, singing *villotte*, and madrigals, the prince accompanying himself on the lute.   It is not recorded, unfortunately, what the classically-inclined nymphs and sirens of the Bay of Naples thought of this new Orpheus.   They certainly could never have heard any music quite like it before; nor had anyone else for that matter.   A new accent had come into music, a note of tragedy and despair that it had never before known.

Somewhere about the year 1585, an event took

PLATE II

PICTURE OF THE CARAFA FAMILY, IN WHICH IS PORTRAYED
DONA MARIA D'AVALOS

[face p. 10

place which was destined to be the cause of a most terrible tragedy in Carlo's life.   This event was the death of his elder brother Luigi, in virtue of which Carlo became the heir to the title and estates of the house of Gesualdo. It was therefore incumbent upon him to marry and produce descendants unless the direct line was to be extinguished and the estates dispersed.   One can be fairly certain that the idea of marriage was uncongenial to his temperament, for at a time when the nobility were accustomed to marry at an extremely early age, Carlo had remained single until close on thirty.   We are told too, by a contemporary writer, that he cared for nothing but music (*non si diletta d'altro che di musica*).   However, the obligations of his position proved stronger than his personal inclinations, and in 1586 he was married to his first cousin, Donna Maria d'Avalos, who, though only 21, had already been married twice, and, what was essential, " *havea dati segni sufficienti di fecondita*,"[1] as the chronicler Ammirato observes.

All contemporary chroniclers are agreed on one point, namely, the " surprising beauty " of Donna Maria, one of them even going so far as to say that she was reputed to be the most beautiful woman in the kingdom of the Two Sicilies.   This may seem to us somewhat excessive praise if the portrait of her in the picture here produced of the Carafa family in the church of San Domenico Maggiore at Naples is at all like her.   (She is the figure on the right reading a book).   There she seems rather plain and ordinary, as many famous beauties of bygone ages do in their

---

[1] " had already given sufficient proofs of fruitfulness."

portraits. Her first husband, whom she married at the early age of fifteen, was Federico Carafa, son of Ferrante Carafa, Marquis of S. Lucido, " admired by the whole nobility as an angel from Heaven," writes the rapturous and fulsome Ammirato. They had two children, but after three years Federico died suddenly, *"forse per aver troppo reiterare con quella i congiungimenti carnali,"* says another indiscreet chronicler. Two years later the young widow married Don Alfonso, son of the Marquis di Giuliano, who seems to have had a stronger constitution, or at least greater moderation and prudence, for in 1586 a papal dispensation for divorce was granted, followed almost immediately by her marriage to Carlo Gesualdo.

The wedding was celebrated with truly regal magnificence, we are told, and feasting and rejoicing in the palace of San Severo, where the Prince lived, continued for many days.

The marriage appears to have been extremely happy for some three or four years—which seems about as long as Donna Maria could endure one husband—and a son, Don Emmanuele, was born to them. (As we shall see later there was possibly also a second child). And then, in the year 1590 occurred the terrible event in Gesualdo's life to which allusion has been made.

The main sources of our information concerning the tragedy are two; firstly, a chronicle of the time called the MS. Corona; secondly, the *Informatione presa dalla Gran Corte della Vicaria*. With the aid of these two valuable documents we are able to reconstruct the whole drama with considerable accuracy, although, as will be seen, they differ slightly on certain points. The first deals more fully with the events which led up to the tragedy, the second with the tragedy itself. Apart from their biographical relevance to our subject, they also afford us a fascinating insight into the life and manners of the times, and for that reason alone would deserve attention. The translations which follow are by no means literal. I have preferred to sacrifice verbal accuracy to the preservation where possible, of the colour and atmosphere of the originals.

" The enemy of the human race, unable to endure the spectacle of such great love and happiness, such conformity of tastes and desires in two married people, awakened in the bosom of Donna Maria impure desires and a libidinous and unbridled appetite for the sweetnesses of illicit love and for the beauty of a certain knight. This was Fabrizio Carafa, third Duke of Andria and seventh Count of Ruovo, reputed to be the handsomest and most accomplished nobleman of the city, in age not yet arrived at the sixth lustre, in manners so courteous and gracious, and of appearance so exquisite that from his features one would say that he was an Adonis; from his manner and bearing, a Mars. He had already long been married to Donna Maria Carafa, daughter of Don Luigi, Prince of Stigliano, a lady not only of great beauty but also of supreme goodness, by whom he had four children." (It will be noted that the only person in the whole narrative who is not lovely beyond words is our poor Carlo. Donna Maria is the Venus, the Duke of Andria is the Mars, Don Carlo the Vulcan).

" The equality of age in the two lovers, the similarity of their tastes, the numerous occasions

presented by balls and feasts, the equal desire of both
parties to take pleasure in each other, were all tinder
to the fire which burnt in their breasts.   The first
messengers of their mutual flames were their eyes,
which betrayed to their hearts with flashes of lightning
the Etna which each cherished for the other.   From
glances they passed to words, from words to letters,
given to and received by faithful messengers, in which
they invited each other to sweet combat in the lists of
love.   The Archer, though reputed blind, was a very
Argus in finding opportunities for coupling the two
lovers, and knew well how to find a convenient place
of meeting for the first occasion of their coming
together, which was in a garden in the Borgo di Chiaia,
in the pavilion whereof the Duke did lie concealed,
awaiting his beloved who, on pretext of diversion and
entertainment, was taken there.   And she, while walk-
ing there, affected to be overcome by some bodily pain,
and separating herself from her escort, entered into
the pavilion wherein lay the Duke, who, without the
loss of one moment, put into execution the work of
love.   Nor was this the only occasion on which they
came together for these enjoyments, but many and
many times did they do so for many months in various
and diverse places according to the opportunities provided by fortune.   Most frequently it was in the
palace of the Princess, even in her very bedchamber,
through the aid of her maid-servant, that they did
dally amorously together.   This practice, having
become frequent and familiar, came to the ears of
relations and friends of the Prince, amongst others to
those of Don Giulio Gesualdo, uncle of the Prince
Don Carlo.   This Don Giulio had himself been

fiercely enamoured of the charms of Donna Maria, and had left no stone unturned in order to attain his desire; but, having been several times reproached by her for his foolish frenzy and warned that if he persisted in such thoughts and intentions she would divulge all to the Prince her husband, the unhappy Don Giulio, seeing that neither by gifts nor by entreaties nor by tears could he hope to win her to his desires, did cease to importune her, believing her to be a chaste Penelope. But when whispers came to his ears concerning the loves and pleasures of Donna Maria and the Duke, and after that he had assured himself of their truth with his own eyes from more than one certain sign, such was the wrath and fury which assailed him on finding that the strumpet did lie with others, that, without losing one moment of time, he straightway revealed all to the Prince. On hearing such grievous tidings, Don Carlo did at first seem more dead than alive; but, lest he should place credence too lightly in the asseverations of others, he resolved to assure himself of the truth of the matter himself.

In the meanwhile the lovers had been warned that their secret was known, whereupon the Duke gave pause to his pleasures; but Donna Maria, unable to endure this remission, solicited the Duke that they should resume again. He then made known to her that their guilty passion had been detected, and represented to her the dangers to both honour and life which would ensue to both alike if they did not keep their crapulous desires under control.

In reply to these prudent reasonings, the Princess answered that if his heart was capable of fear he had better become a lackey; that nature had erred in creating a knight with the spirit of a woman, and in creating in her a woman with the spirit of a valorous knight. It did not behove him to reveal the vileness and cowardice of a common man, and if he were capable of sheltering fear in his heart he had better chase from out of it his love for her and never come into her presence again.

At this angry reply, which touched him to the very quick, the Duke went in person to the offended lady, and spoke to her as follows:—" Fair lady, if you would that I should die for love of you, I shall be greatly honoured in being the victim of your beauty. I have the courage to meet my death, but not the constancy to endure yours. For if I die, assuredly you will not live. This is my fear which makes me coward; I have not strength to endure this blow. If you see no way to avert a calamity, give me at least the assurance that the Duke of Andria alone will be the victim of your husband's vengeance, and then I shall let you see whether I am afraid of steel. You are too cruel, not to me, who still finds you too merciful, but to your own beauty, in exposing it thus to moulder away before its due time in the darkness and silence of the tomb."

To these words the Princess made answer thus :— " My lord Duke, one moment of your absence is more death-dealing to me than a thousand deaths which might come to me through my delights. If I die with you I shall nevermore be separated from you, but if you go away from me I shall die far apart from all that my heart holds dear, which is your self. Make up your mind, then, either to show yourself faithless by departing from me, or to prove yourself loyal by not abandoning me. As for the reasons which you have given me, you should have taken thought of them before, not when the arrow has sped and it is too late. I have courage enough and strength enough to endure the cold steel, but not the bitter frost of your absence. You had no right to love me, nor I to love you, if we were capable of entertaining such base and cowardly thoughts. To conclude—I so wish and so command, and to my order I brook no reply unless that you would lose me for ever."

To this impassioned speech the unhappy Duke, bowing humbly in token of submission, replied :— " Since you wish to die, I shall die with you; such is your wish, so be it."

And so did they continue in their delights.

The Prince, now alert and on the watch, having had all the locks of the doors in the palace secretly removed or damaged, and particularly those of the rooms wherein the Princess was wont to dally amorously with her paramour, gave out one day his intention of going to the chase, as was his custom, declaring also that he would not return that evening. Accordingly he set out in hunting attire and on horseback, accompanied by a numerous retinue of intimates and followers, and made as if to go to that place known as Gli Astroni, having previously left orders with some of his servants who were privy to the secret, to leave open at night all the necessary doors, but in such wise that they should yet retain the appearance of being closed. Then the Prince took his departure, and went to conceal himself in the house of one of his relations.

The Duke, having learnt that the Prince had departed upon a hunting expedition and would not return that evening, set forth at four hours of the night[1] in search of his usual pleasures, and was received by Donna Maria with her wonted affection. And after that they had solaced themselves at their ease, they fell asleep and thereby lost both body and soul.   For in the meanwhile the Prince, having returned secretly to the palace at midnight, accompanied by a troup of armed men chosen from among his intimates, made his way rapidly to the bedchamber of the Princess, and with one blow broke open the door.   Entering furiously he discovered the lovers in bed together; at which sight the state of mind of the unhappy prince can be imagined.   But quickly shaking off the dejection into which this miserable spectacle had plunged him, he slew with innumerable dagger thrusts the sleepers before they had time to waken.

And after he had ordered that their dead bodies should be dragged from the room and left exposed, he made a statement of his reasons for this butchery, and departed with his familiars to his city of Venosa.

And this tragedy took place on the night of the 16th October, 1590. ⸱ The bodies of the wretched lovers remained exposed all the following morning in the midst of the hall, and all the city flocked to see the pitiful sight.

The lady's wounds were all in the belly, and more particularly in those parts which she ought to have

---

[1] The first hour of the night is 6.30—7.30 by our time. Consequently four hours of the night is 9.30.

kept honest; and the Duke was wounded even more grievously.

Too beautiful, too alike, too unfortunate were this unhappy couple.

At the hour of vespers the bodies were removed for burial amidst the lamentation of the entire city.

Such was the end of impure desires.

That is all we learn from the *Successi tragici et amorosi de Silvio et Ascanio Corona*. The Venetian ambassador to Naples mentions a few other details in one of his communications to his government. After giving a succinct account of the tragedy, he adds that "these three princely families (i.e., Gesualdo, d'Avalos, and Carafa) were intimately connected with and related to almost all the other noble families of the kingdom, and everyone seems stunned by the horror of this event. The illustrious Lord Viceroy himself was greatly dismayed at the news, for he loved and greatly esteemed the Duke as a man who both by nature and through application was the possessor of all the most noble and worthy qualities which appertain to a noble prince and a valorous gentleman. Various ministers of justice, together with officials of the Courts have been to the palace, and after making various inquiries commanded that all persons connected with the case should be sequestered and guarded in their own houses; but up to the present, nothing more has been heard of the matter."

And now we come to the verbatim report of the proceedings of the Grand Court of the Vicaria, a copy of which, by a rare stroke of good fortune, is still extant, although the original document has disappeared from the Neapolitan Archives.

It consists of three separate depositions : first, that of the examining magistrates and officials; secondly, the narrative of the servant-in-waiting to Donna Maria; and thirdly, and most interesting, the evidence of Don Carlo's personal servant.   Many details in these will be found to be at variance with the account given already; where these discrepancies occur, it is only natural that we should give the preference to the official narrative.   For example, the trap laid by the Prince by announcing his intention of going hunting— so reminiscent of the device of the Sultan Schahriar in the " Arabian Nights "—is clearly erroneous.

Informatione presa dalla Gran Corte della Vicaria. Die 27 octobris, 1590, *in quo habitat Don Carolus Gesualdus.*"[1]

" As it has been brought to the notice of the Grand Court of the Vicaria that in the house of the most illustrious Don Carlo Gesualdo, in the place of S. Domenico Maggiore, the illustrious Lady Donna Maria d'Avalos, wife of the said Don Carlo, and the illustrious Don Fabrizio Carafa, Duke of Andria, had been done to death : the illustrious gentlemen Don Giovan Tommaso Salamanca, Fulvio di Costanzo, Royal Councillors and Criminal Judges of the Grand Court, the Magnificent Fiscal Procurator, and I, the undersigned Master of the Grand Court, held conference in the house of the aforesaid Don Carlo Gesualdo.   On entering into the upper apartments of the said house, in the furthest room thereof, was found dead, stretched out upon the ground, the most illustrious Don Fabrizio Carafa, Duke of Andria.   The

---

[1]   Evidence taken by the Grand Court of the Vicaria on the 27th October, 1590, in the house of Don Carlo Gesualdo.

only clothing upon the body was a woman's nightdress, worked with lace, with a collar of black silk and with one sleeve red with blood, and the said Duke of Andria was covered with blood and wounded in many places, as follows : an arquebus wound in the left arm passing from one side of the elbow to the other and also through the breast, the sleeve of the said night-dress being scorched; many and divers wounds in the chest made by sharp steel weapons, also in the arms, in the head, and in the face; and another arquebus wound in the temple above the left eye whence there was an abundant flow of blood. And in the self-same room was found a gilt couch with curtains of green cloth, and within the said bed was found dead the above-mentioned Donna Maria d'Avalos clothed in a night-dress, and the bed was filled with blood. On being seen by the aforesaid gentlemen and by me, the aforesaid Master, the body was recognised to be that of Donna Maria d'Avalos, lying dead with her throat cut; also with a wound in the head, in the right temple, a dagger thrust in the face, more dagger wounds in the right hand and arm, and in the breast and flank two sword thrusts. And on the said bed was found a man's shirt with frilled starched cuffs, and on a chair covered in crimson velvet, near the said bed, was discovered a gauntlet of iron, and an iron glove, burnished; also a pair of breeches of green cloth, a doublet of yellow cloth, a pair of green silk hose, a pair of white cloth pantaloons, and a pair of cloth shoes, all of which vestments were without injury, whether sword thrusts or bloodstains. And at the side of the apartment of the lady, the door of the said room was found to be smashed at the foot and could not be closed by means of the handle, for that the injury was made in such a way that it could not lock, nor would the handle hold when placed in the aperture, and likewise the lock of the door had been bent and twisted in such a way that the key could not enter the keyhole, and consequently the said door could not be locked.

And on entering into the antechamber wherein was the small door opening on to the spiral staircase which led down to the apartment of Don Carlo, Pietro Bardotti, servant in waiting to said Don Carlo Gesualdo, gave up to the said gentlemen a key, saying that when he entered the room where he had found the Lord Duke and Donna Maria d'Avalos lying dead, he found the said key upon a chair beside the bed; and this key, which opened the door of the room of the apartment in the said house, he did declare to be false. And the key being taken by me, hereunder signed Domenico Micene, by order of the above-mentioned gentlemen, the lock of the door in the said room was inspected, and another ordinary key was found in the lock thereof. And on essaying the said key which had been given by the said Pietro, it was found to open the lock of the door in the said room as well as the ordinary key.

And at the same time by order of the said gentlemen, two coffins were brought into the said room, and with them came the Reverend Father Carlo Mastrillo, a Jesuit father, together with two other Jesuit priests. And when they had washed the body of the said Duke of Andria the following wounds were clearly discerned upon him, namely : arquebus wounds in the left arm, through the elbow and in the flank with two shots,

one arquebus wound about the eye from side to side,
some of the brains having come out; and he was also
wounded in many places in the head, face, neck, chest,
stomach, flanks, arms, hands and shoulders—all by
sword thrusts, deep, many of them passing through the
body from front to back. This body had been found
immediately upon entering the said room, three paces
distance from the couch wherein lay the said Donna
Maria d'Avalos. And underneath the said body were
many marks upon the floor made by swords passing
through the said body and penetrating deeply into the
said floor. And after that the said body had been
washed and dressed in a pair of black silk breeches
and a jerkin of black velvet, it was taken by the
Reverend Don Carlo Mastrillo, who had come to
receive the body on behalf of the wife of the said Lord
Duke, the Countess of Ruvo his grandmother, and the
Lord Prior of Ungheria his uncle. And when it had
been placed in a coffin by order of the said illustrious
gentlemen, the body was given to the Jesuit fathers
above mentioned, who placed it in a coach and
departed with it; and the said clothes which were
found upon the chair within the said room, belonging
to the said Duke, together with the gauntlet, glove
and false key, were consigned unto me, the said
Domenico Micene, that I should have them in safe
keeping.

And then there came the illustrious Marchioness di
Vico, the aged aunt of the said Donna Maria d'Avalos,
in order that she might dress her; and after that she
had been dressed by the servants of the house she was
placed in the other coffin and consigned to the care of
the illustrious Lady Duchess of Traietto, according to

the wish and request of the illustrious Lady Sveva Gesualdo, mother of the said Lady Maria, and was carried to the church of S. Domenico.

And further it is attested that the said Lords Justiciary and the Fiscal Lord Advocate, on descending to the apartment on the middle floor wherein the said Don Carlo is alleged to have slept, found in one of the rooms three halberds, one of which had a twisted point, and all three soiled and stained with blood, and also in the same room a round shield of iron, large, and with black silk fringes, a short sword with a silver hilt, a long sword similarly gilt, and two wax torches which had been left behind in the said house.

In witness whereof

> *By order of the above-mentioned illustrious gentlemen, I Dominico Micene, Master of the Grand Court, have written the above account with mine own hand.*
>
> *Evidence examined and taken by me, Master Giovanni Sanchez, with the assistance of Master Mutio Surgenti, fiscal advocate, by order of the Excellent Masters, concerning the death of the illustrious gentleman Don Fabrizio Carafa, Duke of Andria, and of the Lady Maria d'Avalos. The 28th October, 1590, in the house of the illustrious Duke of Torremaggiore, lately inhabited by Don Carlo Gesualdo and Donna Maria d'Avalos.*

Silvia Albana, aged 20, being as she said, maid-servant to the aforesaid Lady Maria d'Avalos, and keeper of her wardrobe and of all things which concerned her person, and having served her mistress for six years, bore witness on oath. On being examined

and questioned, what did witness know concerning
the death of the said Lady Maria d'Avalos, and who
killed her, and in what manner? she answered, that
the truth of what she knew was as follows :—

On the Tuesday evening, which was the 26th day[1]
of the present month, that is, eight days ago, the Lady
Donna Maria, after that she had dined, retired to rest
at about four hours of the night. Witness, together
with one Laura Scala, likewise servant in attendance
on the said Lady, did undress her and left her in bed.
Whereupon Laura then retired to bed, as she was wont
to do, in the room adjoining that wherein the said lady
was reposing, and witness set about preparing her
garments for the next day.

Then did the said Lady Donna Maria call witness
to her; and when she had come into the room, the said
lady asked for clothes wherewith to dress herself.
And in reply to witness's enquiry why she wished to
dress, she made reply that she had heard the whistle
of the Duke of Andria and wished to go to the
window—which witness had seen the lady do many
times before, and on several occasions, when the moon
was shining, she, the witness, had seen the Duke of
Andria in the street. And she did recognise him by
moonlight from having often seen him by daytime,
and knew him well, having often heard him con-
versing with the said lady.

And the said lady having ordered that garments
be brought to her, witness brought forth a petticoat
and a shawl for her head; and the said lady, being
dressed, did go to open the window, and went out

---

[1] Obviously an error of the copyist.

upon the balcony, first ordering the said witness to
stand on guard and to warn her if she should hear any
astir in the house or in the courtyard. And witness
did as she was told; and as Lady Maria opened the
window she heard five hours of the night striking.
After half-an-hour, that is, at five-and-a-half hours of
the night, the said Lady Donna Maria summoned
witness to close the window and to undress her again.
Accordingly witness disrobed her; and when that the
Lady Donna Maria had retired to bed, she ordered
that another night-dress be brought to her, as that
which she was wearing was wet with sweat.   And
witness brought her one which had a collar of worked
black silk and a pair of cuffs of the same colour, and
left it upon the bed as she was commanded to do—
which night-dress witness saw on the Duke of Andria
when she discovered him in the morning, in the very
room wherein the said Lady Donna Maria did sleep,
dead upon the ground, covered with blood, and
wounded in many places.   And after the said Lady
Donna Maria had told her to leave the night-dress
which she had brought upon the bed, she asked that a
candle might be lit and placed upon the chair; and
accordingly witness lit a wax candle and placed it
upon the chair.   And when witness was retiring for
the night the said Lady Donna said to her, " Shut the
door without turning the handle and do not come in,
unless I call you."   And witness did as she was told,
and as the said Lady Donna Maria had told her not
to come in unless she was called, she did not wish to
undress but laid herself down upon her bed fully
attired, and while reading a book fell asleep.

While still asleep she heard the door of the room

wherein she was, which stood at the head of a flight of
stairs leading to the middle floor on which the Lord
Don Carlo Gesualdo did live, violently opened. And
on awakening with a great start it did seem to her as
if she were dreaming and did see, while the lamp in
the room wherein she lay was going out, three men
entering whom witness knew not by sight. And
scarcely had she seen them than they approached the
room wherein slept the said Lady Donna Maria; and
she saw that one of them, who was the last in order,
was carrying a halberd, but could not say if the others
were carrying arms. And speedily the said men
entered into the inner room, and witness heard two
loud reports, and almost at the same moment the
words, " There, it is done." Hardly had she heard
these words spoken than by the staircase she perceived
the Lord Don Carlo Gesualdo, husband of the Lady
Donna Maria, entering the room wherein witness was
sleeping; and together with the said Lord Don Carlo
came Pietro Bardotti with two lighted torches in his
hands. And the said Lord Don Carlo was carrying a
halberd, and said to witness, " Traitress, I shall kill
you. This time you shall not escape me." And
having ordered the said Pietro Bardotti not to permit
her to depart, he entered into the room of the said
Lady Donna Maria. And as he went in, he ordered
the said Pietro Bardotti to fix one of the torches which
he was carrying at the side of the door. The said
Pietro did so, whereat witness fled into the room
where the child was, and, lingering there a moment,
did hear the said Don Carlo in the room saying,
" Where are they?" And the nurse besought him
that for the love of God he would not do hurt to the

child. Whereupon the Lord Don Carlo having commanded that the closet in which the lady was wont to keep her jewels should be closed, went out. Then witness, hearing no sounds proceeding from the room, came out from under the bed where she had been hiding and saw the above-mentioned Pietro Bardotti with a lighted torch. And he said to her, " Do not fear, Don Carlo has departed." And on witness asking him what had happened, Bardotti replied, " Both of them are dead."

Witness had not the courage to enter the room until the morning, when the other servants came up and it was already light; and then they did all go in together and saw the Lady Donna Maria d'Avalos lying dead with many wounds, in her own bed, upon which lay a man's shirt, and on a chair near the bed a pair of green silk knee-breeches, a pair of stockings, and white underclothing; and near the door a dead body with many wounds and covered with blood; and on coming close she recognised it to be the body of the Duke of Andria.

And such was the evidence of witness, who added that the Duke was wearing the lady's nightdress.

On being asked if she could say whether the clothes which were upon the chair were soiled, and to whom they belonged, witness answered that the clothes which she saw were unsoiled and unspotted, and that she believed them to belong to the Duke of Andria, but could not say for certain.

On being asked what time it would have been when the three men of whom she spoke, and Don Carlo after them, came up the staircase, witness replied that when she came out from under the bed, as told above, the clock struck seven.

On being asked whether she knew the whereabouts of Don Carlo Gesualdo, and who had gone with him, witness replied that she did not know, because from the time when they left until Don Giovanni came thither with the other Lords Justiciary and the Fiscal Lord Advocate, she had been kept shut up in the women's apartments, and had not spoken with anyone.

On being asked what had happened to the body of Donna Maria, she said that on the Wednesday morning the Marchioness di Vico had come and had had the body dressed, and witness had helped in so doing; and thus dressed, the body had been placed in a coffin, and she understood that it had been taken to the church of S. Domenico. And this was all she knew. And being asked how the Duke gained entrance, she answered that she did not know.

Silvia Albana bore witness as above.

On the same day and in the same place, Pietro Malitiale, otherwise Bardotti, aged about forty, said that he was in the service of the Lord Don Carlo Gesualdo as a personal servant, and that he had served the family for twenty-eight years. Giving evidence on oath, he was questioned concerning the occurrence and his knowledge thereof, firstly, where at present was Don Carlo, and how long was it since he had seen him? He answered that at the moment he did not know where he was, and that he had not seen him since the Tuesday evening, a week past; and that on the Wednesday morning, when he left, it would be about seven hours of the night. He had

departed on horseback, but witness himself did not
see his departure.

On being asked why Don Carlo left that night,
and with whom he had gone, he replied : " My Lords,
I shall tell you the truth.   On the Tuesday evening,
which was the 26th day of the present month, the said
Lord Don Carlo dined at three hours of the night in
his apartments on the middle floor, undressed himself, and retired to bed as he was wont to do every
evening; and those who served him at supper were
witness, Pietro de Vicario, a man servant, Alessandro
Abruzzese, and a young priest who was a musician.
And when he had finished dinner the aforesaid Pietro
de Vicario and the others departed while witness
remained behind to lock the door.   After he had
secured the door the Lord Don Carlo composed himself to slumber, and witness covered him up and,
after undressing, went to bed.   Being thus asleep, it
would be about six hours of the night when he heard
the Lord Don Carlo calling for him that he should
bring him a glass of water.   Witness went to the well
to draw water, and when he had descended to the
courtyard he noticed that the postern gate, opening on
to the street, was open at that late hour.   And on
taking up the water he beheld Don Carlo up and
dressed in doublet and hose.   And he told witness to
give him also his long cloak to put on.   When witness
asked him whither he was going at such a late hour of
the night, he replied that he was going a-hunting;
and on witness observing that it was not the time for
going to the chase, the said Lord Don Carlo replied
to him : " You shall see what hunting I am going to
do."   So saying he finished dressing, and told witness

to light two torches; which done, the said Lord Don Carlo drew from beneath the bed a curved sword which he gave to witness to carry under his arm, also a dagger and a poignard together with an arquebus. Taking with him all these weapons, he went to the staircase which led up to the apartment of the Lady Donna Maria d'Avalos, and while mounting by it the said Lord Don Carlo spoke to the witness, saying : " I am going to massacre the Duke of Andria and that strumpet Donna Maria." And while mounting the stairs, witness saw three men each of whom was carrying a halberd and an arquebus; which men, witness attested, threw open the door at the head of the stairs which led to the apartments of Donna Maria. And when the three men had entered into the said apartment of Donna Maria, the Lord Don Carlo said to them : " Slay that scoundrel together with that strumpet ! Shall a Gesualdo be made a cuckold?" (*A casa Gesualdo corna*). Then witness heard the sound of firearms, but heard no voices, because he had remained outside the room. After that he had remained a short while thus, the three men came out, and he recognised one of them to be Pietro de Vicario, man-servant, another to be Ascanio Lama, and the third to be a confidential servant called Francesco; and they departed by the same staircase by which they had come up armed. Then Don Carlo himself came out, his hands covered with blood; but he turned back and re-entered the chamber of Donna Maria, saying : " I do not believe they are dead." Then the said witness entered with a torch and perceived a dead body near the door. The said Don Carlo went up to the bed of the Lady Donna Maria and dealt her still

more wounds, saying : " I do not believe she is dead."
He then commanded witness not to let the women
scream, and the said Lord Don Carlo Gesualdo
descended the staircase by which he had come; and
witness heard a great noise of horses below, and in the
morning saw neither the Lord Don Carlo, nor his confidential servant, nor any of the members of the Court
or of the household of the Lord Don Carlo.

And this is that which the witness knew.

Signum crucis.

So ends the *Informatione preso dalla Gran Corte
della Vicaria.*   The copyist of the document adds
that the inquiry was discontinued at the command of
the Viceroy, in view of the manifest justification for
the Prince's act in slaying the Duke of Andria and his
own erring spouse.   But this would seem merely to
be a personal opinion of the scribe, and not at all in
accordance with the general sentiment which, as we
shall see, was ranged almost unanimously on the side
of the guilty pair.

Other accounts of this terrible deed are to be
found, with slightly varying details, in the minor
literature of the time, but none of them are so
authentic or circumstantial as the two above reproduced.   Mention, however, should be made of the
version of Brantôme in his celebrated *chronique
scandaleuse*, the *Vies des Dames Galantes (Discours
premier, sur les dames qui font l'amour et leurs maris
cocus).*   After describing the occurrence with many
inaccuracies, he adds that :—

" Il y eut des parens de ladite dame morte qui en
furent très-dolents et très-estomacqués, jusques à s'en
vouloir ressentir par la mort et le meurtre, ainsi que la

loy du pays le porte, mais d'autant qu'elle avoit esté tuée par des marauts de valets et esclaves qui ne méritoient d'avoir leurs mains teintes d'un si beau et si noble sang, et sur ce seul sujet s'en vouloient ressentir et rechercher le mary, fust par justice ou autrement, et non s'il eust fait le coup luy-mesme de sa propre main; car n'en fust esté autre chose, ny recherché.

" Voilà une sotte et bizarre opinion et formalisation, dont je m'en rapporte à nos grand discoureurs et bons jurisconsultes, pour sçavoir, quel acte est plus énorme, de tuer sa femme de sa propre main qui l'a tante aimé, ou de celle d'un maraut esclave.

" Il y a force raisons à déduire là-dessus, dont je me passeray de les alléguer, craignant qu'elles soyent trop foibles au prix de celles de ces grands.

" J'ay ouy conter que le viceroy, en sçachant la conjuration, en advertit l'amant, voire l'amante; mais telle estoit leur destinée, qui se devoit ainsi finer par si belles amours.

" Cette dame estoit fille de dom Carlo d'Avalos, second frère du marquis de Pescayre, auquel, si on eust fait un pareil tour en aucunes de ses amours que je sçay, il y a long-temps qu'il fust esté mort."[1]

Another and greater French writer, Anatole France, made the tragic occurrence the subject of one

---

[1] There were some among the relatives of the said lady who were deeply grieved and offended thereat, even to the point of wishing to revenge themselves by death and murder, according to the laws of the country; all the more because she had been done to death by knaves and servants whose hands were unworthy to shed such fair and noble blood, and for this reason alone they would have had vengeance upon the husband, either by law or otherwise, and not if he had dealt the stroke with his own hand; but nought came of it.

Here indeed is a crazy and extravagant notion, concerning which I invite the judgment of our great lawyers and good jurisconsults: namely, whether of his finest short stories, entitled "*Histoire de Doña Maria d'Avalos et de Don Fabricio Duc d'Andria.*" It is to be found in the volume entitled *Le Puits de Sainte Claire*, but as it is almost entirely a work of imagination it does not concern us here.

The Sansevero palace in the Piazza San Domenico where the tragic event took place, still exists, although the great earthquake of 1688 which devastated Naples necessitated its restoration. Through the kindness of Sig. Salvatore di Giacomo, however, I am fortunately able to reproduce here a contemporary painting which shows the palace as it was at the time when it was inhabited by Gesualdo.

It is related that after the flight of the Prince, the palace was closed and remained unoccupied for a considerable time; but that every night at the hour of midnight the people who lived in the vicinity would hear a loud and anguished cry, and the white phantom of Donna Maria would be seen gliding in the darkness through the alleys and passages which surrounded the palace. To this very day the story is told among the common people of Naples, and the palace has never lost its sinister reputation. In recent times the sudden collapse of part of the building, involving loss of life, was at once attributed to the

---

it is more monstrous to kill the wife you have loved by your own hand or by that of a vile lackey.

Many arguments can be brought forward on this score which I will forbear to mention, fearing that they should seem trivial beside those of such eminent persons.

I have heard it said that the Viceroy warned her and her lover on hearing of the plot which was afoot ; but such was their destiny, and the fated end of such sweet loves.

This lady was daughter to Don Carlo d'Avalos, second brother of the Marquis of Pescara, who would himself have long been dead if any such misfortune had befallen him in any of his amours of which I have heard tell."

[*face p. 34*

PALAZZO SAN SEVERO BEFORE EARTHQUAKE OF 1688

working of a fatal curse which has rested on it throughout the three centuries and more that have passed since the events which we have been narrating took place.

There was another and later inhabitant of the palace, however, to whom part at least of this evil reputation must be ascribed. This was Signor Raimondo di Sangro, Prince of San Severo, who lived there about the middle of the 18th century. He seems to have dabbled in science, or alchemy; and during his occupation of the palace wandering tongues of flame and infernal lights were often seen to flicker through the windows on the ground floor, which look out on the Vico Sansevero—and sometimes the flames were red, sometimes blue, or even a lurid green, and strange sounds also were to be heard. In the vivid and superstitious imagination of the Neapolitan *lazzarone*, this Prince is represented as a kind of Nostradamus or magician who possessed the power of raising the dead and of fasting indefinitely. He is also said to have been accustomed to drive about over the sea in a carriage drawn by supernatural horses.

But to return to Gesualdo. He went straight to the Viceroy, Don Giovanni Zuniga, Count of Miranda, and acquainted him with what had happened. The Viceroy advised him to put himself out of reach of the relations of the murdered couple, who belonged to two of the richest and most powerful families of the kingdom. The Prince therefore retired to his castle at Gesualdo, which he proceeded to fortify against a possible attack. Indeed, such was his fear of vengeance that he even went so far as to cut down all the forests and thickets which stood around his stronghold, lest they should serve to conceal the approach of hostile forces.

These precautions were not by any means superfluous. The nobility of that time, we are told by a contemporary writer, " were arrogant and presumptuous, greatly disposed to vengeance," and particular examples of the length to which affronted honour or *amour propre* would go are so numerous as to be almost commonplace.

" The exaggerated insistence on the point of honour resulted in many deeds of violence, in brutal and callous murders on the slightest pretext. . . . The Marchese di Polignac was imprisoned for venturing to challenge so exalted a person as the Prince of Salerno, who had insulted him. But this was not enough for the outraged Prince. One morning the Marchese, hearing a loud noise, rushed to his window to see what had happened, and was instantly shot dead by a hired bravo. The noise had been made by the Prince's orders. Elaborate duels were fought for the most absurd reasons. Thus a pet dog belonging to the Principessa di Montaguti was stolen by a maid and sold to a Spinelli, who refused to return it. He was challenged by her son, and in the duel which followed, eight combatants fought on each side. The whole party caroused together till daybreak when —*ripigliati gli sdegni*—they proceeded to the Piazza Vittoria to fight. One of them was killed, and the rest took refuge in the neighbouring churches. The other side only succeeded in wounding a Prince Pietrapasia, who retired to his villa at Posilipo. One day a boatload of the friends of the dead man rowed round to the villa, and on his appearance opened fire on him, but failed to hit him."[1]

In such a highly irascible age it was obviously well to take some precautions against possible reprisals of a similar nature. But Gesualdo had even more particular reasons to be on his guard against an attempt at revenge. The murdered Duke had a certain nephew called Fra Giulio Carafa, who, to say the least, seems to have been of a somewhat impulsive disposition. It is related of him that one fine day a certain poet, named Giovan Battista Arcuccio, was passing along the street, reciting his own poems as he went, in a state of lyrical exaltation, at the top of his voice. Fra Giulio Carafa, who happened to be standing at the time in front of his house, requested him to speak in a slightly more subdued tone. A few heated words ensued, after which the gentle friar, raising aloft the stick which he was carrying, smote the unfortunate poet upon the head and killed him. It is possible that the particular poem he was reciting was a very bad one, but even so the death penalty seems to us somewhat excessive. What might not Fra Giulio do under stronger provocation? One trembles in anticipation for the luckless Prince; but, as it happened, Fra Giulio, having as we have seen, avenged the perpetration of a poem by committing a murder, proceded now to avenge a murder by writing a poem—a sonnet in which he abused our friend the Prince in the most vehement language:

> *O barbaro crudel fier omicida*
> *Di te stesso ministro e di vergogna,*

---

[1] *Times Literary Supplement*, August 7th, 1924. Leading article, " Naples under the Viceroys."

Il fuggir si lontan che ti bisogna?
Forse, morto il buon Duca, ancor ti snida?
Già non te segue Astrea, anzi ti affida
Più di quel che tua mente stolta agogna.
Che temi dunque? forse ti rampogna
Lo spirto invitto suo, forse ti sgrida?
Esser ben può, poi che l'offesa grave
Fu troppo, mentre avea nudo il suo petto :
Con molt' armi troncasti il suo bel stame.
Qual ragion vuol che le tue macchie lave
Sangue sparso per man di gente infame
Se errasti tu, che mal guardasti il letto?[1]

Altogether the affair caused the shedding of a great deal of innocent verse. All the poets of Naples, from the great Tasso down to the obscurest rhymester of the age, seem to have burst out into a simultaneous howl of anguish over the fate of the two unfortunate lovers. A large number of these lamentations have been preserved, and though not always, or even generally, of high poetic value, they nevertheless possess a certain interest for us. In all of them, without a single exception, the sympathies are entirely on the side of the lovers; even Tasso, whose close friendship with Gesualdo, one would have thought, might have inclined him to take a different view, mourns the sad fate of the two unhappy lovers without seeming to reprove their conduct. But this is only in accordance with the spirit of the time, which regarded

---

[1] " O barbarous, cruel and savage murderer, to your own self minister of shame, what need have you to fly away so far? Although the good Duke is dead, still thou fleest? Already Astrea ceases to pursue you, and even grants you more than which your foolish mind desires. What then is it that you fear? Perchance his unconquered spirit causes you remorse, perchance reviles you. It might well be so, since the offence was too grave ; seeing that when he was defenceless, with many weapons you severed the thread of his life. How could you think that blood poured out by the hands of vile creatures could wash out your dishonour while you were straying, and caring so little to keep your couch inviolate?"

with a complaisance bordering almost on tacit approval, the infidelity of wives. This point of view is perhaps best summed up in the words of Bartolomeo Gottifredo, in his treatise called *Specchio d'Amore*, where he judges " Piene di gentilezza, di cortesia, e d'umanità una giovane, la quale ai dolci preghi d'un amante, commossa, e da' suoi martiri, pietosa divenuta, del suo fedel servire finalmente degno premio gli dona."[1]   There is hardly even a suggestion of justification for Gesualdo's act; " impious assassin " is the politest thing said about him.   All the sympathies are for Mars and Venus, none for the outraged Vulcan.

There is, however, one poem worth reproducing here, not for its poetic merits, which are slight, but because it sheds a certain light on Gesualdo's character.   This is a sonnet by one Scipione Teodoro :

Tosto che l'armi e l'omicida ha scorto
Del consorte crudel che occide e fiede
La bella donna, che l'amante vede
Dest'in un punto, et assalito, e morto;
—Ahi, crudo—disse—tu spregiasti a torto
Le mie bellezze, e chi con ferma fede
Amolle, uccidi, ond' or poca mercede
Viver me fia, se la mia vita hai morto.
Qui tace e mort'attende; odio e dispetto
Vincon pieta; se rende ella al furore
Del ferro e del morir mostra diletto.
Sol con la bella man ricopre il core,
Quasi spregi la vita e pregi il petto,
Ove col caro amante alberga amore.[2]

---

[1] " abounding in kindness, courtesy, and humanity is the young woman who, moved by the soft entreaties of her lover and taking pity upon his torments, finally bestows upon him the worthy recompense of his devotion."

[2] As soon as the fair lady did perceive the murderous arms of the cruel spouse who smites and slays, and her lover assailed and dead, she spoke as follows :—' Ah, cruel one, you did wrongfully despise my charms, and now you have killed him who with firm faith cherished me ; whence

—the suggestion being that Gesualdo, after a few years of married life had ceased to care for his wife, and had neglected her. And this may very well be true, in view of what we already know of his temperament and inclinations. What then could be more natural than that the young and beautiful Donna Maria should turn to someone who was better able to appreciate her charms?

The Duke of Andria's infatuation for her can equally well be explained. His wife, we are told, was excessively religious, and " porto troppo nelle feste l'austerita della vita devota." When she retired to a nunnery after her husband's death she had to be given a cell apart from the rest, because " aveva l'anima cosi infiammata, che gliene ridondava l'ardore anche nel corpo—e le grida e i sospiri che dava fuori eran si gagliardi, da turbar la quiete e il sonno delle altre."[1] Little wonder then, if the Duke should prefer to sleep elsewhere than in the marital couch.

But we have not yet reached the end of this unhappy story. It is recorded that, on his arrival at Gesualdo, the Prince's fury and resentment had not yet wholly spent themselves. It seems that, in addition to the son Emmanuele, who had been left behind in Naples, Donna Maria had presented him with another child, who was then only a few months old. Believing that he recognised in its features a

---

life is now of little consequence to me, seeing that my life is dead.' With this she is silent; hatred and scorn overcome pity : she yields to the fury of the steel and shows delight in death. Only with her fair hand she shields her heart, as though she scorned her life and prized the breast that harboured love and her dear loved one."

[1] " her soul was in such an inflamed condition, that her ardour communicated itself to her body, and the shouts and sighs which she gave forth were of such vivacity as to disturb the peace and slumber of all the others."

PLATE IV

PICTURE IN CONVENTO DEI CAPPUCCINI AT GESUALDO

[face p. 40

PLATE II

resemblance to the Duke of Andria, he had the cradle, and within it the unfortunate child, suspended by means of silk ropes attached to the four corners of the ceiling in the large hall of his castle. He then commanded the cradle to be subjected to " violent undulatory movements," until the infant, unable to draw breath, " rendered up its innocent soul to God."

This ferocious act seems to have appeased the Prince's wrath. In later years, overcome by remorse for his triple crime, he caused a monastery to be built at Gesualdo in expiation of it. This monastery, the Convento dei Cappuccini, still exists, and in the church attached to it there hangs a painting of surpassing interest to us, seeing that it contains a portrait of the Prince, which is here reproduced for the first time.

At the top and in the centre of the picture the Redeemer is sitting in judgment, His right hand upraised in the act of pardoning the guilty and contrite Prince who is kneeling humbly in the lower left-hand side of the painting. On his right is sitting the Blessed Virgin Mary, who, with her right hand, is pointing to the sinner for whom she is interceding. On the left hand of the Saviour stands the archangel Michael who, with the right hand, is similarly pointing to Gesualdo for whom he is imploring pardon. Slightly lower down, on the left side of the picture is Saint Francis, with both arms and hands outstretched in an attitude of supplication for the repentant sinner; and opposite to him is Saint Domenic, likewise invoking the Divine Mercy. Below Francis is the Magdalene, the vessel of perfume at her side, who with her face turned towards Gesualdo, seems to be

exhorting him to trust in the Divine mercy of Our
Lord whom she indicates to Don Carlo with both
hands.   Similarly, opposite to her is Saint Catherine
of Siena, looking up towards the Redeemer and pointing
out to him the suppliant sinner.   Finally, in the lower
section of the painting is the Prince himself, dressed
in the Spanish fashion, kneeling bareheaded, while
Saint Carlo Borromeo, Archbishop of Milan—his
maternal uncle, by the way—attired in his Cardinal's
robes, places his right arm protectingly on his erring
nephew's shoulder, with his face turned towards the
Divine Redeemer in the act of presenting him.
Opposite, on the right, kneels a Franciscan nun with
her hands raised in a gesture of supplication, whose
identity is somewhat uncertain, though she is
undoubtedly intended to represent some member of
the family.   Catone, in his *Memorie Gesualdine*,
believes it to be Donna Eleonora d'Este, the Prince's
second wife (whom he erroneously considers to be his
first wife); but it is more probably Isabella, sister of
Carlo Borromeo, who became a nun with the name of
Sister Corona, thus explaining the crown which she
wears upon her head.   In the middle of the picture is
a beautiful *bambino*, representing the murdered child,
with two angels at his side, while below, unfortunately
hidden from sight by the altar, are two souls burning
in eternal flames, which are, needless to say, intended
to represent Donna Maria and the Duke of Andria.

It must be admitted that the portrait of the Prince
contained in this picture makes a curiously disagree-
able impression on one.   It is not necessary to know
anything of his life to detect in these long, narrow,
slanting eyes with their delicate but strongly marked

eyebrows, in the small, puckered, and sensual mouth, aquiline nose, and slightly receding forehead and chin, a character of the utmost perversity, cruelty and vindictiveness. At the same time it is a weak rather than a strong face—almost feminine, in fact. Physically he is the very type of the degenerate descendant of a long aristocratic line.

It is not known how long Carlo remained at Gesualdo, but in 1591 his father died, and he consequently became Prince of Venosa. Some reconciliation with the relatives of the murdered couple must, however, have been effected, for Tasso wrote to him at Naples a letter dated 19th April, 1592. From this time onwards, Gesualdo's life is essentially one of intense pre-occupation with music. True, he married again, as I have said, Donna Eleonora d'Este, in 1594, but this was done probably more for dynastic considerations than from inclination—like his first marriage, in fact. She seems to have been a very virtuous lady, however, for there is no record of his having killed her. She survived him many years, and it is just possible that she murdered him.

However that may be, we next hear of Gesualdo at the Court of the Estes, his second wife's family, at Ferrara, in 1594. At that time Ferrara was the most cultured, enlightened, and splendid city in the whole of Italy. Indeed, one might say that Ferrara dominated the closing period of the Renaissance in Italy, as Florence dominated its early stages; the Medici were the wet-nurses, the Estensi were the undertakers. With Ferrara are associated the last great writers of the Renaissance—Ariosto, Tasso, Guarini, and others of less importance individually, but nevertheless forming a brilliant constellation, such as Alberto Tollio, Cinthio, Patricio, Salviati, and Pigna.

Life at the court of the last Duke, Alfonso II, was as near an approach to paradise as is permitted to mere mortals. Describing it, Annibale Romei says in the *Discorsi* : " It was more like a royal court than that of a grand duke; for not only was it full of noble lords and valorous cavaliers, but it was also a meeting-place of the most learned and cultured spirits, and of men pre-eminent in every calling. This Prince (Alfonso II), truly admirable in all his acts, so skilfully blended business with pleasure, and so carefully apportioned both, that he did not allow himself to be wearied either by too many serious occupations or by too great a surfeit of diversions. Consequently his Grace has arranged all things in their proper season, such as, at the time of Carnival, masks, joustings, feasts, comedies, concerts, and other similar recreations, which are enjoyed in such peace and harmony that it is indeed a joy and a marvel to observe on such occasions the happiness of our city."

And so the pleasure-loving and perhaps slightly effeminate Ferrarese, in such striking contrast to the energetic and virile Florentines, were content to remain aloof from the ceaseless turmoil and intrigue of contemporary politics, and to pass the last fleeting and irretrievable moments of the Renaissance in the splendid gardens of the Belvidere, with its groves ot cypresses and plane-trees, its cool grottoes, rose gardens, and marble pavilions with their frescoed walls, among the orange and olive trees and vineyards, the air heavy with the mingled fragrance of jasmine and orange-blossom : or by the side of artificial lakes whose fish had learnt to glide close to the surface of the water at the sound of a small silver bell, listening for hours on end to the stately and harmonious discourse of scholars, philosophers, and poets, and to the endless discussions so dear to the Renaissance mind, concerning beauty, truth, virtue, nobility, and so forth; and in the summer heats they would retire into *villeggiatura* at Comacchio or in the forests of Mesola where the Duke, like the fabulous Kubla Khan, had built a vast palace surrounded by twelve miles of walls enclosing numerous hunting lodges, deer parks, and marble pavilions. There they would spend the long days in hunting the wild boar, or in the chase with falcons or with hounds, and in every form of amusement which human ingenuity could devise, or the heart of man desire.

But more especially was Ferrara a city of music, the art which above all others had always been assiduously cultivated there, and in the exercise of which Ferrara had always excelled all the other cities of Italy. In the palace of the Grand Duke, according to the testimony of Ercole Bottringari, there were concerts several times every day, sometimes performed by as many as 57 singers—an unprecedented number in those days. Instruments were kept constantly in tune by musicians specially maintained for the purpose, so that they could be taken up and played at a moment's notice. Instruments were made there, and the musical library was reputed to be the most extensive in the world, both in printed books and in manuscripts. And just as the Medici were themselves poets and scholars, so the princes of the Casa d'Este did not merely content themselves with favouring, protecting, and maintaining musicians at their own expense, but also practised the art themselves. From records of the times we learn that they were in the habit of procuring the most eminent professors of music available for the instruction of their children; even the pages and gentlemen-in-waiting received musical instruction, and it was rare indeed to find a gentleman at their court who was not at the same time a cultured musician.

This musical education and culture was by no means confined to the male sex. "*Rarissime furon le donne che non cantassero suonassero*," and Lucrezia d'Este, afterwards Duchess of Urbino, was a veritable melomaniac. Even the nunneries were musical centres; in addition to their devotional duties, all the nuns cultivated music assiduously and frequently gave musical *soirées* which were often attended by the whole court. Some of them even composed. One, Olimpia Leoni, was celebrated for her exquisite contralto voice and her viol playing; another, Raffaella Aleotti, for her extemporisations upon the organ and her compositions, many of which were published. Even Benvenuto Cellini, who cordially detested music, could not refrain from praising the music and musicians of Ferrara.

Moreover, all the most eminent composers of the day, and of earlier days, were connected, directly or indirectly, with Ferrara. Brumel was *maestro di cappella* there; so was the great Josquin Desprès, who wrote there one of his most celebrated works, called after Duke Ercole II the *Missa Hercules Dux Ferrariae;* so likewise were Vicentino, Cipriano de

Rore, Luzzasco Luzzaschi[1], and the brothers Alfonso and Francesco della Viola, all of whom spent the greàter part of their active careers at Ferrara. Willaert, the maestro of San Marco in Venice, had close relations with the Estensi, to whom he presented many of his compositions. Orlando di Lasso visited Ferrara twice, in 1567 and in 1585; Luca Marenzio was *maestro di cappella* to the Cardinal Ippolito d'Este; so likewise was Palestrina himself, who also passed several years at Ferrara, and John Dowland visited the court some time between 1585 and 1595.

It is, moreover, a highly significant fact that the poets who, more than any others, were associated with the great vogue and popularity of the madrigal (the form most cultivated by musicians of the time apart from church music)—namely, Tasso and Guarini—were all their lives intimately connected with the court of Ferrara. Another and even more important association concerns the introduction of solo singing, an innovation ascribed in all musical histories to Vincenzo Galilei, who made a setting of the Ugolino scene from Dante's *Inferno* with accompaniment of a viol about 1585, though there is evidence to show that the experiment was made, at least ten years earlier, at Ferrara, by one Vincenzo Giustiniani. When we also take into account the fact that the school of Ferrara was the one most closely identified with daring harmonic experiments, it will readily be seen that when the history of music comes to be re-

---

[1] Luzzaschi was a pupil of Cipriano da Rore and the master of Frescobaldi. He knew Gesualdo and dedicated his fifth book of madrigals to him (1594). For particulars of Luzzaschi's remarkable madrigals for a solo voice with instrumental accompaniment, see O. Kinkeldey, *Sammelb. d. int. Musik-Gesell.* IX.

written—and the sooner it is the better—it will be found that the Ferrarese played an infinitely greater part in the idiomatic evolution of modern music than the little group of literary *dilettanti* and musical amateurs who frequented the house of Count Bardi in Florence, in the last years of the sixteenth century. In any case, the works of Peri and Caccini are devoid of any intrinsic musical interest, and are only historically important, which cannot be said of those of the madrigalists at the court of Ferrara.

It was accordingly to this musicians' paradise that the Prince of Venosa bent his steps.   The date of his advent there is uncertain; we know only that he must have found the life and atmosphere highly congenial, for he rented the spacious palace of Marco Pio, in the Strada degli Angeli, and settled down there.   He intervened with the Duke on behalf of his friend and *protegé* Tasso, who, though he had formerly disgraced himself by his insane exploits and behaviour at the court, desired to be forgiven and received back once more.   The request, however, was not acceded to; in any case it would probably have been too late, for the unhappy poet died in 1595.   Duke Alfonso II died two years later without leaving any heirs, and the city passed into the hands of the Popes.   With him died the Italian Renaissance; the sunset or after-glow which had shed such a dazzling radiance died out, giving place to the all-pervading twilight of the Catholic Revival, or Counter-Reformation.   All the former glory of the city departed, never to return; the palaces were deserted and gradually crumbled away into ruins, and the Belvidere gardens became a desolate wilderness—the *"deserta bellezza di Ferrara"*

PLATE V

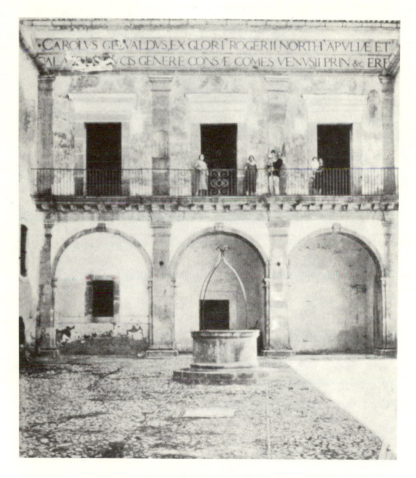

COURTYARD OF THE CASTLE AT GESUALDO

of which a later poet, Gabriele d'Annunzio, sings. All the courtiers departed. Only Marfisa d'Este remained, the lovely maenad of whom Tasso had sung when she led the revels with flushed cheeks and unbound golden hair, now grown old and grey, her thoughts occupied only with religion.

Gesualdo probably lingered on for some years after the death of the Duke; he seems then to have returned to Naples or to Gesualdo. His closing years seem to have been unhappy, if we are to trust the evidence of a chronicle entitled *Rovine di Case Napolitane del suo tempo*, by one Don Ferrante della Marra (Duca della Guardia nell' anno 1632).

" The Prince Don Carlo Gesualdo lived to see his crimes punished by God through the infliction of four great misfortunes, resulting in the total extermination of his house and race.

" The first of these was that he did suffer great shame for the space of two years, owing to the conduct of Donna Maria d'Avalos, his wife, in lying with Don Fabrizio Carafa, the Duke of Andria, almost every night, practically within sight of her husband.

" Having slain Donna Maria, by whom he had a son Don Emmanuele, Don Carlo became frenzied (*si pose Don Carlo a freneticare*) and began to treat his vassals not only avariciously and lasciviously, but also tyrannically; and owing to this, the anger of God being aroused against him, he lost a beautiful male child whom he had by Donna Eleonora d'Este, sister of the Duke of Modena, who was his first wife (the usual error—Donna Eleonora was his second wife), and this was his second great affliction.

" The third misfortune was that through the

agency of God, he was assailed and afflicted by a vast
horde of demons which gave him no peace for many
days on end unless ten or twelve young men, whom
he kept specially for the purpose, were to beat him
violently three times a day, during which operation he
was wont to smile joyfully.   And in this state did he
die miserably at Gesualdo, but not until he had lived
to witness, for his fourth affliction, the death of his
only son Don Emmanuele, who hated his father and
had longed for his death, and, what was worse, this
son died without leaving any children save only two
daughters whom he had by Donna Polisena of
Fustemberg (Furstenburg?), a German princess.[1]

" And although he had arranged that the elder of
these should marry within the family, his house suffered
two more misfortunes.   Firstly, against his express
dispositions the young Princess of Venosa was
married, by order of the King, to Prince Nicolino
Ludovisio, nephew of the Pope, Gregory XV; and at
this day she doth live at Bologna, having caused the
loss to her family of the principality of Venosa, and
also the state of Gesualdo which had been in the
family for little less than six hundred years.
" The second of these two other misfortunes—and
to my thinking, greater than all the others—was that
after the death of Don Emmanuele, the Princess
Polisena went to live with her aunt, the second wife of
the Prince of Caserta, Andrea Matteo Acquaviva;
and having lived thus for many years did acquire
an evil reputation, for not only was she all this time

---

[1] Concerning Don Emmanuele, we are told that he was a poet and
greatly interested in astrology (*Borzelli—Maria d'Avalos*, p. 96.)

concubine to the said Prince, but had secretly had several children by him.

" Thus did it please God to destroy, both in possessions and in honour, a princely house which was descended from the ancient Norman kings."

This is indeed a gloomy picture, and in spite of its undoubted exaggerations, conveys nevertheless a strong impression of authenticity. I have taken the trouble to verify the facts concerning the extinction of the House of Gesualdo, and have found the narrative strictly accurate in its details. Even the more fantastic statements, such as that concerning the horde of demons, receive striking and unexpected confirmation from a reference to Gesualdo which is to be found in a work of Thomas Campanella " *Medicinalium juxta propria principia* " (lib. III, art. 12). The writer, in attributing to flagellation the virtue of curing intestinal obstructions, adduces in proof of his assertion the case of Gesualdo : " Princeps Venusiae musica clarissimus nostro tempore cacare non poterat, nisi verberatus a servo ad id adscito.'"

In other words, what Ferrante della Marra calls demons, we to-day would call auto-intoxication; it is simply a matter of terminology. And, after all, does not modern medical science regard this unfortunate complaint with as much fear and superstition as our predecessors regarded demons? Is it not, in fact, believed to be the source of all the ills to which mortal flesh is subject—the Evil One himself?

Dr. Ferdinand Keiner, in his excellent little

---

[1] " The Prince of Venosa, one of the best musicians of his age, was unable to go to the stool, without having been previously flogged by a valet kept expressly for the purpose." Thomas Campanellæ, *Medicinalium juxta propria*, Libri tertii, cap. III., Art. XII. : (" Monstrosa cura.")

brochure *Die Madrigale Gesualdos von Venosa*, suggests that the prevailing melancholy of Gesualdo's music might be attributed to the tragic circumstances of his married life.   It seems, however, much more likely that it was caused by the distressing and almost universal complaint from which he suffered.   Burton, in his great work, the "*Anatomy of Melancholy*" Part 1, Sect. 2, Memb. 2, Subs. 4) declares "that costiveness and keeping in of our ordinary excrements is a cause of many diseases, and of melancholy in particular," and supports his assertion with many concrete examples and expert medical opinions.

Carlo Gesualdo seems to have died in 1613 (not 1614 as Keiner and others say), for there is in existence a will made by him, dated 3rd September, 1613, and opened by his wife, Donna Eleonora, on the 29th of the same month and year.   Unfortunately I have not been able to obtain a copy of this interesting document.   Modestino, in his book *Della Dimora di Torquato Tasso in Napoli* (Naples, 1863), quotes from it, saying that he made a copy from the original in the State Archives, which so far I have been unable to trace.

In it, Modestino tells us, the Prince invokes the intercession on his behalf of the saints represented in the picture here reproduced.   He left 40,000 ducats yearly to his widow for as long as she remained unmarried and continued to reside within the kingdom of Naples.   If she did not wish to live in Gesualdo, she was given the choice of the castle at Taurasi or the palace at Naples on the shore between Mergellina and Posilippo.   We learn also that he had a natural son, Don Antonio Gesualdo, to whom he left 50 ducats monthly for the duration of his life.

This will contradicts the statement of another writer, Litta, in his *Famiglie Celebri d'Italia*, where we are told that Donna Eleonora did not live long in harmony with the Prince, her husband. Complaining principally of his extreme prodigality, she petitioned the Pope for a divorce and obtained it, after which she retired to Modena, and she entered the convent of Santa Eufemia, where she died in 1637. This is obviously wrong, however.

Gesualdo was buried in the chapel of Saint Ignatius in the church of the Gesù Nuovo at Naples. The inscription on his tomb was as follows :—

CAROLUS GESUALDUS

COMPSAE COMES, VENUSIAE PRINCEPS,

SANCTI CAROLI BORROMEI SORORE GENITUS,

CELESTI CLARIOR COGNATIONE

QUAM REGIUM SANGUINE NORTMANNORUM

SEPULCRALI DUO HAC ARA SIBI SUISQUE ERECTA

COGNATOS CINERES, CINERI FOVET SUO,

DONEC UNA SECUM ANIMENTUR AD VITAM,

SOCIETAS IESU SIBI SUPERSTET, AC POSTERA

INTEGRE PIETATIS

OCULATA SEMPER TESTIS MEMOR.

P.

Nothing of the tomb remains. After the earthquake of 1688 the Gesù Nuovo was rebuilt and in the process the sepulchre of Gesualdo disappeared.

And this is all we know concerning the life of that most singular and delectable gentleman, His most

Illustrious and Serene Highness Don Carlo, third Prince of Venosa, eighth Count of Consa, fifteenth Lord of Gesualdo, Marquis of Laino, Rotondo, and S. Stefano, Duke of Caggiano, Lord of Frigento, Acquaputida, Paterno, S. Manco, Boneto, Luceria, S. Lupolo, etc.

Pray for his soul.

APPENDIX I

LETTERS FROM TORQUATO TASSO TO DON CARLO GESUALDO, PRINCE OF VENOSA

(i) APRIL 19TH, 1592.

Once again I entertain the hope that your Excellency will be coming to Rome before Christmas. . . . I send you herewith ten madrigals following the others, begging you to excuse their poverty of invention, occasioned by natural infirmity and unfortunate circumstances; in spite of which, with the utmost difficulty, and solely in order to please your Excellency, I have forced myself to adopt new forms, as behoves the poet, who—according to Aristotle—must either be divine, or of a pliant and versatile disposition. I kiss your Excellency's hand.

(II) APRIL, 1592.

I have taken this fresh opportunity of writing to your Excellency this very same week concerning the lack of finish in one of the madrigals which I had sent you, of which I now send you again a new version, together with a few others, beseeching you to tolerate my negligence or inadvertence as others have tolerated them in former days less adverse to me. Of your coming I should at least like to be certain, since I am in ignorance of all your other plans. To the Cardinal Gesualdo I desire to be warmly recommended by your Excellency.

(III) DECEMBER 10TH, 1592.

The replies of your Excellency, like your favours, can never come too late, so greatly do they resemble

all divine things which demand time for their fulfil-
ment; but if your silence is to be construed as a sign
of your pending advent to Rome, I can the more
readily console my disappointment with it, and with
the hopes of your favours.   I send you herewith
another ten madrigals, and I would have sent you an
even greater number, but having lost them like money,
and perhaps in much the same way, I am compelled to
re-write them.   Nevertheless there ought to be altogether up to the present time about forty; and if I
write to you thus it is because I would not have myself
seem excessively idle to your Excellency, and because
I would wish you the sooner to recognise my poverty
of invention.   I am reading Neapolitan history at
present, but I long for greater novelty and times either
more remote or more recent.   I have sometimes
wished that I could do similar things myself, but as it
happens, I am not considered worthy of the task,
whereat I greatly grieve; because in the leisure of the
Vatican, if I could have arrived there through the good
graces of His Holiness, I should not have been
obliged to undertake other tasks.   I have had the
desire to call around me the amorous muses, and have
not yet repented of the desire.   But I do beseech your
Excellency to pardon me if I am not able to dwell
with them any longer for the present, though perhaps
I shall be permitted to call them to me again.   I kiss
your hand.

P.S.—If it would not displease your Excellency
to have the madrigals re-copied, the following two
lines of the last could be re-written thus :

In erto colle, in una valle o'n selva
Non s'ode augello o belva.

(IV) ROME, DECEMBER, 1592.

Repeated experience has made me ashamed of myself and of my feeble invention, so reluctant to recover itself, and so poor in the reproduction of the innumerable aspects of beauty; therefore I beseech your Excellency not to desire further demonstrations of my culpability. It contents me well that you do not deceive yourself with false notions concerning my ignorance and insufficiency; be only certain of the affection I bear you, and of the desire I entertain for your favours. . . . Your Excellency cannot doubt that I love you and honour you as much as is permitted by your high station in life and my lowly one; although I may not be able to satisfy you in the composition of the five madrigals which I herewith send to you. The first, which are of exactly the character and style which you desire, possess no rare qualities. In the others I am myself inclined to censure the hidden erudition. I do not deceive myself in so slight a matter of art, though possibly it is suitable to the character of the poems.

We are now at the Christmas festivities, and I, with my usual infirmity, suffer terribly from the cold in this city, and pray God to console me through the grace of His Holiness and of all these illustrious gentlemen; and more particularly through the benevolence of the Cardinal Gesualdo and your Excellency, of whose goodness and nobility I do not wish to despair."

(V) JUNE, 1594.

Since I rejoiced with your Excellency on the occasion of your marriage, and with a few stanzas demonstrated to the best of my ability my devotion and respects, I have come to Naples with the intention of purging myself, and have already commenced the treatment. May it please God that it will benefit me sufficiently to enable me to survive until the return of your Excellency. In the meanwhile, if you are in any way able to help me or do me any favour, know that it is well merited on account of my great affection and esteem. In expectation of your gracious favours and those of your uncle, the Cardinal, I kiss your hand.

BIBLIOGRAPHY

*(The following list does not represent all the books
consulted in writing the foregoing life of Gesualdo,
but only a few of the more important).*

Aldimari, Biagio. Historia genealogica della Famiglia Carafa,
  1691.
Ammirato, S.   Delle Famiglie nobili Napoletane, 1651.
Arienzo, Niccolo d'.   Un Predecessore di Alessandro
  Scarlatti, 1892.
Borzelli, Angelo.   Maria d'Avalos, 1914.
Brantome, Pierre Bourdeille de.   Vies des Dames galantes,
  1822.
Capasso, B.   Torquato Tasso a Napoli, 1895.
Catone, Giacomo.   Memorie Gesualdine, 1840.
Cerreto, Scipione.   Della prattica musica vocale e
  strumentale, 1601.
Crollalanza, G.   Dizionario storico-blasonico, 1886.
Florimo, Francesco.   La Scuola musicale di Napoli, 1880.
France, Anatole.   Le puits de Sainte Claire (Histoire de
  Doña Maria d'Avalos).
Frizzi, A.   Memorie per la storia di Ferrara, 1847-50.
Giacomo, Salvatore di.   Celebrità Napoletane, 1896.
Guerra, Scipione.   Diurnali, 1891.
Keiner, Ferdinand.   Die Madrigale Gesualdos von Venosa,
  1914.
Lellis, Carlo di.   Discorsi delle Famiglie nobili del Regno di
  Napoli, 1674-71.
Litta, Pompeo.   Celebre Famiglie Italiane, 1819, etc.
Masucci, Antonio.   Il Teatro dell' Amicizia, 1661.
Maurel, André.   Quinze jours à Naples, 1921.
Modestino, Carlo.   Della dimora di Torquato Tasso in
  Napoli, 1863.
Mutinelli, Fabio.   Storia arcana e aneddotica d'Italia, 1856.
Napoli Nobilissima, edited by S. di Giacomo, 1892, etc.
Pietri, Francesco di.   Historia Napoletana, 1634.
Ricca, E.   La Nobiltà delle due Sicile, 1859.

Serassi, P. A.   Vita di Torquato Tasso, 1858.
Sitwell, Sacheverell.   Southern Baroque Art, 1923.
Solerti, Angelo.   Vita di Torquato Tasso, 1895.
———————— Ferrara e la Corta estense, 1891.
Summonte, Historia della città e regno di Napoli, 1602.
Tasso, Torquato.   Lettere (edited by C. Guasti), 1852-5.
Valdrighi, F.   Cappelle, Concerte, e Musiche di Casa d'Este, 1884.
Valle, Pietro della.   Della musica dell' età nostra, 1635.
Villa Rosa, Marchese di.   Memorie dei compositori del regno di Napoli, 1840.

ICONOGRAPHY

I.—Painting in the Convento dei Cappuccini at Gesualdo.

II.—A marble bust mentioned and described by Catone in his *Memorie Gesualdine,* and formerly belonging to him. " On the head is to be observed a circlet representing the small crown proper to the rank of a Count, adorned with small embossments denoting precious stones.   Below this the hair is divided into two tresses on either side which are drawn symmetrically together behind the head, meeting below the shoulders.   The neck is adorned with a necklace from which a small cross hangs."   But neither the bust nor its present owner can be traced.

Thirdly, for the sake of ccmpleteness, may be mentioned a portrait in the Conservatorio di S. Pietro a Majella, said to be that of the Prince ; but Sig. Salvatore di Giacomo, who has seen it, assures me that it is not genuine, and bears no resemblance to the indubitably authentic portrait in the picture at Gesualdo.

C. G.

PART II

—

Carlo Gesualdo considered as a Murderer

PART II

—

Carlo Gesualdo considered as a Murderer

Before embarking upon a critical disquisition concerning the merits and faults of Don Carlo's achievement as a murderer, it will first of all be necessary to lay down a few general principles and standards of taste and judgment; and as it was the first pre-occupation of our distinguished predecessor in this particular field of æsthetics, namely, Thomas de Quincey, emphatically to dissociate the art of murder from all moral implications, so it must likewise be ours. It is true, of course, that a murder can, and perhaps should, be considered from a moral standpoint, and from the point of view of society, like any other art; but that is rather the business of the philosophers and moralists, not of æstheticians. Plato, and many other thinkers after him, have concluded that all art is immoral, and all artists a menace to the safety and well-being of the state. He may very well be right; but the fact remains that the work of art exists, and it is the business of the æsthetic critic to consider it scientifically and objectively as a pure phenomenon. We cannot do better than quote here a passage from De Quincey's great masterpiece, " On Murder, Considered as one of the Fine Arts," in illustration of this important point.

"When a murder is in the paulo-post-futurum tense—not done, not even (according to modern purism) *being* done, but only going to be done—and a rumour of it comes to our ears, by all means let us treat it morally.   But suppose it over and done, and that you can say of it, Τετελεσται : It is finished, or (in that adamantine molossus of Medea) εἴργασται: Done it is : it is a *fait accompli;* suppose the poor murdered man to be out of his pain, and the rascal that did it off like a shot, nobody knows whither; suppose, lastly, that we have done our best, by putting out our legs, to trip up the fellow in his flight, but all to no purpose—' abiit, evasit, excessit, erupit,' etc.—why, then I say, what's the use of any more virtue?   Enough has been given to morality; now comes the turn of Taste and the Fine Arts.   A sad thing it was, no doubt, very sad; but *we* can't mend it.   Therefore let us make the best of a bad matter; and, as it is impossible to hammer anything out of it for moral purposes, let us treat it æsthetically, and see if it will turn to account in that way. . . We dry up our tears, and have the satisfaction, perhaps, to discover that a transaction, which, morally considered, was shocking, and without a leg to stand on, when tried by the principles of Taste, turns out to be a very meritorious performance."

The logic and general rightness of this reasoning can hardly be disputed by even the most fanatical moralist, and we are consequently at liberty to pursue our æsthetic investigations without any qualms of conscience.

But, it may be objected here, what pretensions has murder to be considered an art at all?   This ques-

PLATE VI

VIEW OF GESUALDO WITH CASTLE

[face p. 64

tion must be answered at the outset. It is true that
it is not a creative art, as the other arts are; it is in
fact, a destructive, perhaps, indeed, the only destructive
art. One hears a great deal about " the art of war,"
but this is only a manner of speaking, for the more
it tends to become an art, as it was at the time of the
Italian Renaissance, or in China, the more it tends
to eliminate bloodshed. It was considered permissible
to knock your opponent off his horse and take him
prisoner, but bad form and unprofessional conduct to
kill him, unless by an unavoidable accident. It is
possible even to-day to execute a masterpiece of war-
like art without the loss of a man on either side. But
it is manifestly impossible to commit a murder without bloodshed. The essential feature of a murder
lies in destruction; in war it is only incidental.

Yet if this were all that there was to it, murder
could not possibly claim to be an art. But it cannot
sufficiently be emphasised that, to quote again the
admirable words of De Quincey, " Something more
goes to the composition of a fine murder than two
blockheads to kill and be killed—a knife—a purse—
and a dark lane. Design, gentlemen, grouping,
light and shade, poetry, sentiment, are now deemed
indispensable to attempts of this nature." In other
words, blood may be a necessary condition of the art ;
it is the medium in which the artist works, like sound,
colour, line, stone, words : that is all. What finally and
decisively justifies the claim of murder to be considered
an art is, as with all the other arts, its emotional
appeal; its function is, in the Aristotelean phrase, to
purge the soul by means of pity and terror. What
else is drama, indeed, tragic drama, except the

criticism of murder? And this brings us to an interesting point. The criticism of a creative art is essentially destructive, the criticism of a destructive art is creative. One might even say the dramatist bears the same relation to the murderer that the executant does to the composer. It may be observed that when the dramatist invents an imaginary murder on which to base his play, it never has the same inevitability or the same appeal. It is like the composition of a pianist or a violinist. One of the reasons of the supremacy of the ancient Greek and Elizabethan dramatists lies precisely in the fact that they did not try to invent murders of their own, but founded their plays on actual historical murders. Whenever they tried to dispense with this condition, like Cyril Tourneur in *The Revenger's Tragedy*, the result, however fine the poetry, is never wholly satisfactory. It is a great mistake to suppose that it is only the poetry that makes a great tragedy. In the same way we are apt to imagine that a great pianist or violinist is responsible for the beauty of a work. He only realises and adds to the composer's conception, that is all. Similarly the dramatist may reveal a beauty or a terror of which we were not aware in the original murder, but he does not actually create them in the strict sense of the word. Yet there is no doubt that the murderer needs the poet or the dramatist to complete his work, in the same way that the composer needs the executant to give life to his conception. The composer writes the work down on paper, but it does not properly exist without the executant; the murderer executes first, but his achievement has to be written down and re-created by the poet in order to

attain immortality.   Unless he is fortunate in finding
a great writer his murder, however faultlessly
executed, will soon be forgotten.   Where are the
crimes of yester-year?   Their memory lives for a
week in the newspapers, and then fades away entirely.

This has been the melancholy fate of the great
achievement of Gesualdo in the field of murder, as
well as in the field of music.   He has never found, as
he deserved, a Shelley or a Webster to make a *Cenci*
or a *Duchess of Malfi* out of him; and he is equally
ignored and neglected by our choirs and choral
societies.

Incidentally, does not the fact that the murderer
thus provides the material for great works of art go
a long way towards providing a moral justification for
his act?   Without him there would be no *Macbeth*, no
Hamlet, no *Medea, Oedipus, Agamemnon*, etc.   And
is it not the essence, perhaps the main motive, in
committing a murder, to acquire some form of
immortality not otherwise obtainable?   This is certainly borne out by the theories of many psychological
experts, who believe that the desire for notoriety and
fame at any cost is responsible for at least a
large proportion of murders.   And when one
remembers, too, that the murderer's victims also share
in his immortality, can we not say that he deserves
their undying gratitude—or rather their dying
gratitude?

In fact, " To hear people talk," says De Quincey,
" you would suppose that all the disadvantages and
inconveniences were on the side of being murdered,
and that there were none at all in *not* being
murdered."

Let us, however, dismiss all these moral considerations and turn our attention to the work itself, applying to it the critical standards laid down by De Quincey. In the first place, he says, the person murdered ought to be a good man, because otherwise he might perhaps himself be contemplating murder at the very time. This may seem to us to be oversubtle, but a moment's reflection will suffice to convince us of its fundamental justice. For example, a duel resulting in the death of one of the combatants cannot properly be considered a murder; unpreparedness in the victim is essential, the actual " goodness " being immaterial. This condition is amply fulfilled in Gesualdo's case.

Secondly, says De Quincey, the person selected should not be a public character. Everyone will agree to that. A political assassination—for that is generally all it amounts to—can hardly claim to be the highest form of the art. In fact, it is a kind of " programme murder." Charlotte Corday, for example, may be technically a murderess, but that is all. The moment a murderer feels abstract justification for his act, or that warm, genial, self-righteous feeling which so many people experienced in the years of the war, then murder simply becomes a semi-legal execution in the public interest, or a mere " taking the law into one's own hands."

It must be admitted that this question of motive is a most difficult thing to decide. No hard and fast rule can be laid down here; each case has to be judged on its own merits. De Quincey gives us no help on this point. On the whole he clearly tends in the direction of purism and preciosity, a kind of 1890

" murder for murder's sake," for the sheer craftsman's
joy and the creative, or rather destructive, ecstasy, of
the proceeding. His friend's murder of the cataleptic
baker of Mannheim sufficiently indicates his predi-
lections. Personally I find this too precious and
æsthetical. On the other hand it must be admitted
that murder for robbery's sake, for example, is not
sufficiently removed from necessity; for it is only
when an activity is pursued without relation to the
necessities of actual life that it becomes art.

On the whole, I think a nice balance is struck in
Gesualdo's work between these two pernicious
extremes. He had indeed a certain motive but not
sufficient to justify murder. I know that many con-
noisseurs of deservedly weighty reputation would
class the *crime passionel* as a lower branch of the art
of murder, a kind of justifiable homicide. This is the
French school of thought, and their taste is largely
shared by Latin peoples generally at the present day.
But it was not always so; contrary to expectations, it
was not so in Gesualdo's time. Indeed, as we have
seen, sentiment in general was definitely on the side
of the lovers, and against the avenging and affronted
husband.

Another necessary condition of a good murder is
that the perpetrator should not as a consequence of the
times in which he lived, or as a result of his eminent
position, enjoy complete immunity from the conse-
quences of his action. If the perpetrator runs no risk
whatever of losing his life, all art is at an end;
murder ceases to have any significance as soon as one
is in a position to kill anyone who happens to annoy
one, with absolute impunity. Again, contrary to

expectations, Gesualdo was not in such a position, despite his exalted rank, as we have seen from his flight and prolonged absence from the scene of his exploit. Moreover, one of the Venetian ambassadors to Naples about this time, Michele Suriano, considered it one of the defects of the viceregal government that affairs of justice were executed without making any distinction between nobles and common people—a defect because punishment means so little to a mere commoner, and so much to a nobleman.

Whether we agree with this characteristically Renaissance point of view or not, it would at any rate seem certain that Gesualdo ran as much risk of answering for his action as any common subject. On the other hand it must be admitted that the government of Naples in all times has looked with a tolerant and kindly eye upon practitioners of the difficult and exacting art of murder. Even to-day, I believe, there is a higher ratio of murders committed there than in any other European city. Naples may have little to show for itself in other fields of art, compared with other Italian cities such as Florence, Rome, Venice, Siena; but none of them can dispute her pre-eminence in murder. This tolerance and tacit approval on the part of the authorities has had both advantages and defects. It certainly permits of a very high level of technique and execution which, however, is apt to degenerate into facile virtuosity and sterile repetition. It is the opposite with us at the present day. Whether rightly or wrongly, murder is discouraged and looked upon with great disfavour in this country, with the inevitable result that, however fine and striking our productions may be in conception, the lack of facilities

PLATE VII

THE CASTLE AT GESUALDO

[face p. 70

for performance is so great that there is always considerable weakness and uncertainty in execution. These two contrary faults—of sterile virtuosity and amateurishness—are equally avoided by Gesualdo. Both in conception and in execution his achievement is faultless. It might be objected, however, that he left most of the work to his servants to execute, and that therefore he cannot claim credit for it, but this, I think, is a modern prejudice. All the great Renaissance artists employed skilled assistants in order to carry out their conceptions, and in this Gesualdo was only a child of his age. His servants were only instruments which he employed for his æsthetic purposes, as the architect employs bricklayers and so forth.

Another objection that may perhaps be raised to his work is that, in De Quincey's words, it lacks entirely " the grand feature of mystery, which in one shape or another ought to colour every judicious attempt at murder." Here I take leave to differ from my illustrious predecessor. He seems to me to be carried away here by personal prejudice and native sympathies. We northern peoples are inclined to look for certain qualities in a work of art to the detriment or exclusion of others; we are apt to be prejudiced in favour of the romantic element in art. In the southern schools one must look for other qualities; the element of mystery and romance is not to be found there. Gesualdo's murder is essentially Latin; it is full of the light gaiety and vivacious *tempo* of the southern school.

In execution, too, it is quite in the best classic tradition. Cold steel he employs as the basis of his style, as the classical composers used the strings; fire-arms, which might be likened to the brass, he uses sparingly.   In fact it is an open question whether we moderns have not lost more than we have gained through the perfection of firearms, as modern composers have through the perfection of brass.   In these days of six-chambered revolvers we are apt to rely too. exclusively upon this medium, with a resultant monotony and a too constant richness of style.   Any incompetent amateur can make quite a fine display with a revolver, but he would be quite lost if it were taken away from him and a toasting-fork or a tin-opener given to him instead.   Gesualdo handles the firearms with commendable restraint, but with enormous effect.   Not one shot does he waste, as we see from the coroner's inquest.   On the other hand, the figuration of the steel weapons is exceedingly elaborate and complex.   Wooden instruments he neglects entirely; this is perhaps the only conspicuous defect of the work.   A few judicious blows with a bludgeon impart a variety, expressiveness, and rich charm, which cannot be attained in any other way. On the whole he perhaps tends to use too many instruments; his work is a trifle thickly scored here and there.

But all this is carping criticism.   What we can all unreservedly admire is the boldness of conception, the breadth of style, the absolute sureness of execution. There is nothing improvisatory about it; all the effects are foreseen and carefully planned.   It is in the grand manner, and fit to be placed side by side and compared with the best examples of the art, which, by the way, all date from about this period.   The late

Renaissance is indeed the classical age of murder; at no other time does one find such a brilliant constellation of examples, all of so uniform an excellence. It was an age in which the practice of the art was not as yet confined to any particular class of society; in other words it had not yet become professionalised. Even creative artists, philosophers, and scholars, were not averse to dabbling occasionally in the destructive art. The poet Chiabrera murdered a Roman gentleman in revenge for an insult; the historian Davila also committed a murder and was himself assassinated; Tasso, in his periodic fits of frenzy, was wont to attack people with a dagger; Murtola and Marini were in the habit of shooting at each other; and Giuseppe Ortale, a Sicilian poet, was known as the " Cavaliere sanguinario " for his bloodthirsty tendencies.

But more particularly is there a definite connection between music and murder, although it may not be readily apparent. Not that many musicians have actually committed murders (apart from Gesualdo, one can only think of Salieri who, as everyone knows, poisoned Mozart); nor, strange to say, have many musicians been murdered themselves, except Mozart and Stradella. The connection between the two activities is much more subtle but none the less close. In the first place, the significant fact should be noted that the beginning of the decline of murder as an art dates from precisely the same period as the development of music as a personal expression, i.e., the beginning of the 17th century. In the middle ages music was more a craft than an art, because the emotions which we now express in music were then actually expressed in life. In these good old days one committed a murder if one felt like it, and thought no more about the matter; to-day we write an *Elektra* or a *Cavalleria Rusticana* instead, in order to work off our feelings.   In definite relation to the increased difficulties attendant upon the practice of murder, music has become more and more sadistic.   In place of inflicting the utmost pain on a single individual,. we outrage the ears of thousands.

And so we find in the particular case in question. It was not until Gesualdo gave up murder that he seriously took to composing.   His early works are comparatively conventional in style because he was expressing his emotions in another medium.   This fact opens up several fascinating speculations; for example, may not the badness of Mr. ——'s music be accounted for by his over-indulgence in murder? Cannot the present reaction against emotionalism in music be traced to a similar cause, and to the *catharsis* effected by the war?   These, however, are questions which could only be answered at great length, and this is manifestly not the place or occasion for such an ambitious attempt.   My only purpose here is to point out that Gesualdo's eminence in the art of murder is no less than it is in the art of music, and that his achievement in both spheres has been unduly and undeservedly neglected.

PART III

—

Gesualdo the Musician

PART III

—

Gesualdo the Musician

I

Gesualdo, the eminent madrigalist,
Played the lute well, and was not a bad regalist.[1]
At keyboard extemporaries
He beat all his contemporaries,
As, later, did also a lad we call Liszt.

Unlike the Prince Consort of pious memory, Gesualdo was something very much more than an aristocratic virtuoso who dabbled in musical composition. He is not only a figure of paramount importance in musical history, but also a composer whose best work, when all historical considerations are laid aside, still has the power to move us by its intrinsic beauty. After three centuries he is seen to hold a proud place in the distinguished company of those great men whose music was the crowning glory of the Renaissance; and although he stands a little aloof from the great tradition which gave England her Byrd and Italy her Palestrina, yet, as we shall see in the present study, through Luca Marenzio—the sweetness of whose songs had earned him the title of " the swan of Italy "—he joins hands with both. He is by no means an isolated · person of eccentric genius, but rather the fine flower of a school of daringly imagina-

---

[1] Regal : a small portable organ.

77

tive experimental composers. Already, in the middle of the sixteenth century, the polyphonic tradition had ceased to satisfy some musicians. The old order of music was breaking up; composers were becoming discontented with the traditional forms and the arbitrary limitations of the text-books, and were eagerly searching in every direction for new methods of expression. A great deal of the music of the period was merely tentative, the result of practical experiment, of "objective investigation of aural phenomena" (to quote a modern tag) and as such, of no artistic value. But this research work has its use and can always be turned to good account by the man who is big enough to use it as a means to an end and not regard it as an all-sufficient end in itself. Viewing music as a whole, the contributions of experimental composers may be regarded as sketch-books and notes, insignificant in themselves but of the utmost value to the man of genius who is able to develop the resources which these but suggest, and to make use of them as a means of expression. Now Gesualdo was just such a man of genius. " Such a man," as Ambros says in his *History of Music*, " seeks and finds new paths while the men of mediocre talent go plodding safely and comfortably along in the old ruts. Madrigals of average merit according to the old rules were composed by the thousand at this period, and those that time has not devoured are not worth looking at, whereas Gesualdo arouses our keenest interest and sympathy."

The complete silence of practically all English writers on music since Burney and Hawkins on the subject of this intensely interesting composer is

PLATE VIII

FRONTISPIECE OF SACRAE CANTIONES, FIRST BOOK, BY CARLO GESUALDO

rendered the more inexplicable by the profusion of authorities, ancient and modern, who may be consulted in other languages. Sir Hubert Parry, in his volume on the music of the seventeenth century in the *Oxford History of Music*, does not even mention the name of Gesualdo, and Mr. Reginald Lane Poole, in the latest edition of *Grove's Dictionary of Music and Musicians* v. 243) calmly asserts that " of his history nothing is recorded; we only know that he was living in 1613." The only reference[1] to him that I have found in any modern English publication occurs in Dr. Ernest Walker's scholarly *History of Music in England* (1907), where, after citing the Prince of Venosa as " Monteverdi's friend " (an ascription for which there does not seem to be any authority whatever), Dr. Walker remarks that the Madrigal *Moro lasso* "sounds like Wagner gone wrong." The list of " The chief names in musical history " given in Stanford and Forsyth's *History of Music* (1916) includes Steibelt, Sousa, and Saint-Saëns, but there is no mention of Gesualdo, although Mr. Forsyth claims that his list contains all the most important writers of and on music.

The fact is that the important developments in the direction of dramatic music which took place at the beginning of the seventeenth century have somewhat overshadowed the intrinsically musical developments. Historians and other folk whose zeal for classification exceeds their first-hand knowledge of music are accustomed to regard the end of the sixteenth century as the

---

[1] Since these lines were written there has appeared Mr. Ernest Newman's *Musical Critic's Holiday* in which several pages are devoted to a consideration of Gesualdo's work and its appreciation by his contemporaries.

sunset of the polyphonic period, the early years of the
seventeenth as the dawn of the harmonic—and to draw
a rigid line between the two periods.   They make
much of the fact that Caccini called his book of songs
for a solo voice *The New Music*—as though minstrels
and troubadours had not been singing songs to an
instrumental accompaniment for centuries before—
and base Monteverdi's chief claim to remembrance
upon his operatic experiments.   A new form such as
opera—which was in the beginning imposed upon
music from without, not conditioned by an impulse
of purely musical expression—arrests the historian's
attention, even though the music embodied in that
form be of small account in itself; while far more
important, because more intrinsic developments of
musical thought escape its notice simply because they
occur in the course of compositions whose form is more
or less traditional.   Thus it is not so much in the operas
and oratorios of the early seventeeth century that we
find those audacious passages and turns of expression
which seem to foreshadow far more modern methods,
nor yet in those deliberately programmatical pieces for
the virginals on which every musical historian dilates
with such delight, but rather in madrigals and
songs for the voice and lute, pavans and country
dances and scholastic-looking contrapuntal fantasias.

Neither historically nor æsthetically can any
rigid line of distinction be drawn between harmony
and counterpoint, between monody, or homophonic music—that is to say, music with a principal
air or tune supported by a more or less subsidiary
accompaniment — and polyphony, which is the
music of many voices balanced equally one

against another. The florid, dramatically-expressive rhapsodical style of writing for the voice with an instrumental accompaniment was already flourishing in the middle ages, and had already reached a very remarkable degree of excellence in the works of Guillaume de Machault in the thirteenth century. It would hardly be going too far to say that the free declamatory style, usually supposed to be the invention of a little group of late sixteenth-century Italian composers—was the very essence of the secular music of the middle ages. Four square dance-tunes, simply harmonised in four or five parts, can be found by the thousand all through the sixteenth century, and the principal of substituting a lute or viols for such voices as were not at hand had been universally accepted long before Dowland published his first book of Ayres in 1597, " so made that all the parts together, or either of them severally, may be sung to the Lute, Orpherian or Viol de Gambo." And it is interesting to note that Dowland's last book *A Pilgrim's Solace* (1612) is at once the most polyphonic of all his works, and the one which exhibits the most striking and audacious examples of his harmonic invention.

In a sense, both the harmonic and the musico-dramatic experiments of the sixteenth century were influenced by the characteristically Renaissance desire to revive the arts in the forms in which they were practised in ancient Greece, but the experiments undertaken in this spirit resulted in the discovery of something very much more vital than a mere revival of long-forgotten principles. Peri and the other archæologists of Count Bardi's circle, in their anxiety to achieve dramatic verisimilitude, were content to sacrifice most of the elements by which music can be made expressive, whether it be associated with words and action, or not. Monteverdi (as M. Henri Prunières has shown so admirably in his recent book), fired with enthusiasm by their dramatic ideals, was sensible enough to see the folly of sacrificing any of his purely musical resources upon the altar of dramatic truth. He realised that to achieve intensity in the expression of words or situations, his musical resources must be enriched and not impoverished. In this respect Gesualdo may be ranked with him as a composer whose art is firmly rooted in the polyhonic tradition, and whose innovations are in the nature of an exuberant growth from the rich soil of the past, and not, as the works of Peri and Caccini, the dubious and tender first-fruits of a bleak and untilled land.

It is not recorded that Gesualdo played any part in the operatic movement of the period, though it may be confidently assumed that his passionate enthusiasm for music brought him into touch with it at least as a spectator. His fame as a composer rests entirely upon his madrigals, 147 in number, which were published at various dates between 1594 (the year of his second marriage) and 1626.

It appears that, so far from supervising the printing of his works, Gesualdo did not even sanction their publication. The earlier books, at any rate, seem to have been presented to him as surprise packets. It was, of course, a common practice to circulate manuscript copies of musical compositions for many years before their publication was undertaken, and not infrequently a work would be printed for the first time by some unauthorised person from a manuscript copy which was far from accurate. Such, apparently, was the fate of the madrigals contained in what is now known as the Second Book of Gesualdo. These, we learn from Scipione Stella's dedication (though we have no further authority for the statement), were originally published under the strange pseudonym of Gioseppe Pilonij. But, says Stella, "seeing that the press, as is its wont, had made several errors, I, on account of my ardent desire and great obligation to serve you, have taken the trouble to revise them minutely and to correct them with diligence, and to send them to be reprinted by the same press which has already printed another book of your divine madrigals." This dedication is dated June 2nd, 1594. Although no copy of the "Pilonij" madrigals has survived—if, indeed, the book was ever really printed—there is little doubt that the madrigals in question are the earliest of Gesualdo's published compositions. But three weeks before inscribing this corrected edition of them to their real author, Stella had published another collection of Gesualdo's madrigals, apologising, in his dedication of the book to its composer, for having collected and published them. Both volumes were printed by Vittorio Baldini, the ducal printer of Ferrara, and both were issued simply as *Madrigali a Cinque Voci*. It was not until they were reprinted by Angelo Gardano in Venice that they were called the first and second books of madrigals by Gesualdo; and when, ten years later still, they were incorporated in the collected edition printed in score by Giuseppi Pavoni in Genoà, the second book was called the first and the first the second, which seems to prove the priority of the " Pilonij " book in order of composition.   The third and fourth books, both printed by Baldini and published respectively in 1595 and 1596, were sponsored by Hettore Gesualdo.   That these two books were also issued without the composer's authority is clear from the dedications.   Of the madrigals in the fourth book, Hettore remarks : " I have collected them with infinite avidity and, more solicitous for the common good than for your wishes, have sent them to the press.   I shall not, however, as I have done on other occasions, ask your pardon for my zeal, since, if you were disposed to take them away from me, the whole world would come to my defence."   In 1603 two books of *Sacrae Cantiones*, for 5, 6 and 7 voices, were printed in Naples, and in 1611 the book of six-part *Responsoria*, the fifth and sixth books of madrigals appearing in the same year. All these were published by Don Giovanni Pietro Capuccio who tells us that the madrigals of the sixth book were composed in the same years as those of the fifth, " and have therefore been awaited with the utmost impatience by the world for a long time."   We may therefore assume that, in spite of the marked difference in style between these two later books and their predecessors, the interval between books 4 and 5 is not so great as the dates of their respective publication might lead us to suppose.   In 1613 all the six books of madrigals were reprinted in score by Giuseppe Pavoni in Genoa and published under the auspices of Simone Molinaro, *Maestro di Capella* of the cathedral in Genoa, with the following impressive dedication :—

ALLA CONCORDE FAMA
DELLA GENTILEZZA, IMMENSE, INFINITA
INCOMPARABILE DE' CANDIDI AMADORI
DELL' ARMONIA
LIMPIDISS. CRISTALI D'IMMACULATO INGEGNO
HUMILI IN SE STESSI
GLORIOSI IN ALTRI
CIELISTABILISS. DI TRANSPARENTE VERITA
SIMONE MOLINARO
AD ONTA DEL MOLINO TEMPORALE INUINCIBIL DISTRUGGI-
TORE DELLE TERRENE SPERANZE, SACRA QUESTE
CANORE PERLE STILLATE NELLA CONCA DELL'
ETERNA BELLEZZA DA' RAGGI DEL PRENCIPE
DI VENOSA, VENERE NELLA UNION
DELLE GRATIE, E SOLE DELLA
VIRTU MUSICALE.

which, being interpreted, signifies
To the Concordant Fame
Of the Nobility, Immense, Infinite,
Incomparable of pure lovers
Of Harmony,
Limpid crystals of immaculate genius,
Humble in themselves
Glorying in Others,
Celestial, of transparent verity,
Simone Molinaro (Miller)
To the discomfiture of the Mill of time, the invincible
destroyer
Of terrestrial hopes, dedicates these canorous pearls
Distilled in the conch of eternal beauty by the beams
Of the Prince of Venosa, Venus in the
Union of the Graces, and Sun of
Musical virtues.

Of this volume fourteen copies are known to survive, five in Italy, four in England, three in Germany, one in Brussels and one in Vienna.

In Italy, as in England, madrigals were ordinarily published in separate part-books, each voice having a volume to itself. The publication of music in full score was still something of a novelty, and would not have been called for except in the case of a work of quite exceptional difficulty and strangeness; but it shows that the number of people in Italy who were interested in the nature and structure of music, as distinct from those who simply derived pleasure from singing or hearing it, was on the increase. Actually the first score to be published was a collected edition of Cipriano de Rore's four-part madrigals, which was printed in Venice in 1577. On the title-page appear the words : *Tutti i Madrigali di Cipriano de Rore a 4 voci. Spartiti et accomodati per sonar d'ogni sorte d'instromento, et per Qualunque studioso de Contrapunti.* Practically no manuscript scores of any kind have come down to us from this period. To the madrigalists, and indeed to the polyphonic composers generally, a score was simply a rough sketch of a composition, to be thrown away as soon as the separate parts were copied out.

There was only one edition of the Gesualdo score which is, in consequence, an exceedingly rare book. But the various single books of his madrigals were frequently reprinted in parts, both before and after the publication of the collected edition in score, the first, third and fourth books being thrice reprinted, the fifth and sixth twice, and the second no fewer than five times which, if we include the original issue under the name of Giuseppe Pilonij, proves its popularity to have warranted seven editions. Two short and very insignificant madrigals of Gesualdo's which are not included in any other collection appear at the end of Pomponio Nenna's eighth book of madrigals (1618). Finally, twelve years after the composer's death, a collection of twenty six-part madrigals was published by Muzio Effrem, a musician who had been in the Prince's service for twenty-two years. This publication has unfortunately not survived, one part-book only out of the six being extant. That it contained compositions highly characteristic of Gesualdo's later style is evident from a remark of Emil Vogel who appears to have examined the surviving part-book. Particular interest attaches to the dedication of this book, addressed to Gesualdo's widow, Donna Leonora d'Este-Gesualdo, in which Effrem refers to the " perfect and exquisite compositions " contained therein, by reason of the fact that three years previously Effrem had published a violent polemic against Marco da Gagliano (*Censure . . . . sopra il Sesto Libro de Madrigali da Gagliano*) in which he revealed himself as a musician of a distinctly conversative turn of mind, accusing Gagliano of " errors " in his compositions, and of violation of the true principles of counterpoint—a charge surprising enough from one who in the same sentence specifically praises the fifth and sixth books of Gesualdo's madrigals which, he says, Gagliano has plagiarized. Emil Vogel, who has traced resemblances between the fifth and tenth madrigals in Gagliano's book and Gesualdo's *Felicissimo sonno* and *Tu piangi, ò Filli mia*, remarks : " One cannot help wondering how

Effrem came to terms with his conscience over the publication of these six-part madrigals. What a *censure* he could have written, had he wished to be just, about Gesualdo's compositions which surpass by a long way all the censured liberties of Gagliano's! How outraged he must have felt by the exceedingly chromatic madrigal *Sei disposto*! Or was he perhaps paying homage to the principle : *Quod licet Jovi non licet bovi?*"[1]   There can be no doubt that it was to Gesualdo's position and wealth rather than to the intrinsic merits of his music that the more effusive of his admirers paid homage in their written tributes; but when one has made due allowance for a certain amount of snobbishness in the musical public of the time, it is clear that his works achieved a very real and widespread popularity.   Contemporary writers praised him in the most extravagant terms.   For example Josephus Blancanus, in his *Chronologia celebrorum mathematicorum* (1615) refers to him as "Nobilissimus Carolus Gesualdus, Princeps Venusinus, nostrae tempestatis musicorum ac melopoeorum princeps," and continues : " Hic enim rhythmis in musicam revocatis, eos, tum ad cantum, tum ad sonum, modulos adhibuit, ut ceteri omnes musici ei primas libenter detulerint, ejusque modos cantores ac fidicines omnes, reliquis posthabitis ubique avide complectuntur."[2]

---

[1]   There is no reason to suppose, as Eitner does in the *Quellenlexicon,* that the Effrem we are dealing with was not the Mutio Effrem of Bari who contributed to an anthology of *villanelle* by musicians of Bari which was published in 1574.   He would therefore have been an old man at the time of his controversy with Gagliano.   The date of his death is unknown.

[2]   This passage caused Ambros to postulate the existence of certain instrumental compositions of Gesualdo which have not come down to us. It seems more probable, however, that, like so many of his English contemporaries, he wrote music that was " apt for voices or viols "—a view which is corroborated by the title of the Cipriano de Rore score to which

This is certainly an exaggerated statement in one respect, for Gesualdo had no direct imitators or successors, though it is not unreasonable to hold his influence responsible for the harmonic experiments of some of the later monodists such as Saraceni and Belli; but the testimony of Blancanus is by no means an isolated example.

The first English reference to Gesualdo occurs in the chapter on music in *The Compleat Gentleman* of Henry Peacham (1622) where the author, after referring to the musical accomplishments of King Henry the Eighth, says : " The Duke of Venosa, an Italian Prince, in like manner, of late yeares, hath given excellent proofe of his knowledge and love to Musicke, having himselfe composed many rare songs, which I have seene."

Athanasius Kircher, in his *Musurgia* (1650) says that the Prince of Venosa was by universal consent the first to bring music to its present state of excellence, and that all musicians respect and admire him. Doni, who calls him "truly the Prince of modern composers," is at one with a later writer, Archangelo Spagna (*Oratorii overo Melodrammi*: Rome, 1706) in attributing to the influence of Gesualdo many of the later developments of the operatic style, particularly the dramatic recitative and the *affettuoso* manner in musical expression. Later in the eighteenth century

---

reference has already been made. And it is not unlikely, when one considers the formidable difficulties they must have presented to the singers of the period, that Gesualdo's madrigals were performed with some kind of instrumental accompaniment, a conjecture which is supported by the fact that the madrigals in Monteverdi's fifth book (1605) are provided with a figured bass (continuo) in addition to the vocal bass-part. The library of Christ Church, Oxford, contains a manuscript *Basso continuo* part of Gesualdo's first, second, and fourth books of madrigals.

the learned Padre Martini, the friend of Frederick the
Great and one of the earliest admirers of the genius of
Mozart, says that Gesualdo's style " abounds in all
the refinements of art."   A few years later still Sir
John Hawkins, after quoting various authorities in
support of his view, says of Gesualdo : " The
distinguishing excellences of the compositions of this
admirable author are, fine contrivance, original
harmony, and the sweetest modulation conceivable;
and these he possessed in so eminent a degree that one
of the finest musicians that these later times have
known, Mr. Geminiani, has been often heard to
declare that he laid the foundation of his studies in
the works of the Principe de Venosa "—albeit the
influence of Gesualdo is as far to seek in the compositions of Mr. Geminiani as it is in those of " the
celebrated English composer Mr. Purchill" and in the
organ fugues of Handel which a later historian, Orlov,
(*Essai sur l'histoire de la musique en Italie*, 1822)
would have us believe were also indebted to the
Principe.   Hawkins, who seems to have had but a
superficial first-hand acquaintance with the Prince's
music, quotes in full the first two madrigals of the
collected edition (that is, numbers 1 and 2 of Book II.)
on the strength of their having been praised by Kircher
in his *Musurgia universalis* (1650).   Dr. Charles
Burney, on the other hand, though he can find nothing
in Gesualdo's music " except unprincipled modulation, and the perpetual embarrassments and inexperi-
ence of an amateur in the arrangement and filling up
of the parts," at least had the necessary knowledge
and the good sense to select for reproduction in his
General History of Music (1776) the madrigal *Moro*

lasso—one of the finest examples of Gesualdo's mature style—though he characterises it as " extremely shocking and disgusting to the ear," a judgment which seems rather singular by comparison with a sentence which occurs earlier in the same work : " *What kind of music is most pleasing to mankind?* To practised ears, such as has the merit of novelty, added to refinement, and ingenious contrivance; to the ignorant, such as is most familiar and common." But then Burney's view of music in general was rather singular, as is evident from his wonderful definition of the function of the art : " What is Music? An innocent luxury, unnecessary, indeed, to our existence, but a great improvement and gratification of the sense of hearing."

At this point the name of Gesualdo disappears from English musical literature. The Germans, however, begin to pay increasing attention to him. Winterfeld's *Johannes Gabrieli und seines Zeitalter* (1834) contains excerpts from his works and a glowing appreciation of their expressive qualities; the third edition of Ambros's *Geschichte der Musik* (1909) contains, in addition to the detailed account which Ambros gave of him, a new chapter on the rise of chromaticism in Italy by Hugo Leichtentritt; and Theodor Kroyer's *Die Anfänge der Chromatik im Italienischen Madrigal des XVI Jahrhunderts* (1902) and Ferdinand Keiner's monograph *Die Madrigale Gesualdos von Venosa* (1914) provide an immense amount of information about the music of this period which is not to be found in any of the English histories of music.

II

How do we listen to old music and how much of
its import can we assimilate, unsullied by extraneous
associations? We cannot listen ear to ear with its
contemporary hearers. To do so we should have to
project ourselves into our period as fully and as
exclusively as Pirandello's Henry the Fourth. We
should have to forget all subsequent music, and, with
the aid of theoretical treatises, so distort our natural
mentality that all the cumbersome machinery
prescribed by the text-books would have to be
brought into action before we could re-think a passage
with a sixteenth century mind (for we cannot pre-
suppose in ourselves the quality of genius that alone
can surmount such limitations). The appearance of
a D flat would be fraught with hazardous potentialities
and an excursion into B major an adventure into the
heart of an unknown country.

The ears of a modern child are, in a sense, less
innocent than those of a 16th century adult, for a
child's acquaintance with music does not develop
along historical lines. For a modern child the *simplest*
examples of music will be found to date from the
eighteenth or nineteenth centuries; the sixteenth and
the twentieth alike provide some of the most complex.
(This distinction refers merely to the texture of music.
Where appreciation is concerned, the child of to-day
may very likely derive more immediate pleasure from
Ravel than from Haydn).

The modern adult, with a fair knowledge of
music of all periods, cannot without a great effort
listen to old music with other than twentieth century

ears. He is therefore prone to make constant comparison in his mind between the music of the past
and that of his own day, unconsciously or, worse, even
deliberately seeking in it anticipations of later phases
of the art. But this is an æsthetic fallacy, for all old
music was modern once, and it were well if, once and
for all, the habit of classifying music by means of a
sliding scale of " ancient and modern " were dropped.
In all ages there is good music and bad music : music
does not in any sense *progress*, and in no conceivable
respect can the first-rate music of to-day be regarded
as an advance on the first-rate music of the sixteenth
or any other century. But the music of the sixteenth
century has one important if somewhat negative,
point in common with that of the twentieth, and the
reason for the revival of interest in sixteenth century
music at this particular and present period of musical
development is not far to seek. During the past
twenty years we have shed many prejudices and petty
tyrannies of tradition which have hindered our
appreciation of the unfamiliar in music, whether it be
very new or very old; and of these perhaps the most
formidable was the tyranny of that limited tonality
which derives from a too exclusive reliance on tonic-
and-dominant methods. The key system of the
eighteenth and nineteenth centuries, so far from being
an improvement on the older conception of sound-
relations and the perfected goal towards which earlier
musicians had been blindly striving (as the theorists
would have us believe), is but a relic of the decadence
of the modal system which contained within itself all
the potentialities of our major and minor tonality.
The tonality of the key-system is no more than a

limitation imposed upon the freedom of modal writing. The diatonic convention has given us a great deal of magnificent music, but it remains, for all that, a tributary stream, not the main river, of musical development. To ears that are satiated with the diatonic, one of the chief delights of modal music is its quality of unexpectedness which, paradox though it may seem, does not altogether wear off with familiarity.[1]   The absence of key-feeling and the illusion of free and wayward modulation present us with continual surprises; and it is this element of surprise which chromaticism so greatly enhanced. So far from leading modal harmony into the direction of the key-system, it led it rather towards the modern juxtaposition of diatonically remote chords in a sequence that is logically justified by a thread of melody. In polyphonic music we can trace the most surprising twists of harmony to a single semitonic inflection, and careful examination can always reveal a definitely expressive purpose underlying the progression. There can be no doubt that the old composers felt, as we do, that chromaticism quite literally gave *colour* to music.

It is difficult for the modern student of Gesualdo's

---

[1] But we who have been brought up on the diatonic must beware, when first approaching modal music, of mistaking idiom for poetry, and appraising as rare treasures of creative expression passages which represent only the current coin of musical utterance. Anyone reading in a foreign language with which he is but imperfectly acquainted will be frequently in doubt whether a phrase is an image invented by the author or merely a conventional formula of the language.   A writer in *The Times Literary Supplement* recently described the idioms of a language as " a kind of crystallised popular poetry," adding that " many a passage of Chaucer strikes us still as on the borderland between poetry and idiom, as composed of phrases which might have come to him from the lips of the people or might have passed from his lips to theirs." Similarly, many phrases in the plays of J. M. Synge which strike us as being singularly poetical are found to be simply literal translations of Gaelic idiom into English speech.

music to clear his mind of diatonic prejudices sufficiently to appreciate the fact that Gesualdo stands as far away on the other side of the tonic-and-dominant system as certain modern composers, whose idiom may be roughly described as one of modality tempered by chromaticism, stand on this side of it. In many ways the music of the early twentieth century is akin to that of the early seventeenth. Realism, impressionism, tone-painting, experiments in sound-for-sound's sake were then, as now, preoccupations of many composers. Examples abound in the works of Byrd and Dowland and Weelkes and other Englishmen of the time—to go no further afield. It is the twelve-note scale that is the basis of Gesualdo's compositions (in so far as they have, unconsiously enough, a theoretical basis at all) rather than the ecclesiastical modes on the one hand or the diatonic major and minor scales on the other. Most of the speculations of Busoni, in his *New Æsthetic of Music*, and other recent investigations such as those of Alois Haba, on the possible sub-division of the octave into intervals smaller than the semitone, were anticipated by Nicola Vicentino in the middle of the sixteenth century, but neither he nor any of his successors have been able to turn their investigations to any great practical account. Vicentino, with his School of Musical Mysteries, his keyboard instrument, with several manuals, on which each tone is sub-divided into five different notes, and his madrigals that can be sung in five different ways to the same notes (with partial or complete observance of the accidental signs " sharp," " flat," " natural," and "enharmonic dieses," or quarter-tone) was nothing more than an enquiring theorist, an " objective investigator." But Gesualdo was a creative artist whose best works retain their expressive significance to the present day; and since practice is always ahead of theory in musical matters, it is almost impossible for the technical parlance of his day to provide any explanation of the workings of his strange mind. Harmonic analysis in modern terms, such as Keiner has made, is equally useless, if not actually pernicious. It will be far more profitable for those who encounter Gesualdo's music for the first time in these pages to consider it as a purely expressive phenomenon, and to bring as little historical and theoretical prejudice to the study of it as they would bring to the study of their own contemporaries.

Count Bardi and his little coterie of musicians, fired with enthusiasm for Greek art and wishing to resuscitate what they conceived to be the methods of melodic declamation, or recitative as we should now call it, employed in the performance of the ancient Greek drama, set to work and achieved instead the creation of an entirely new kind of music as remote as music could possibly be from ancient Greek practice. Greek music was essentially a melodic art. Neither harmony, as we understand it, nor the combination of independent melodies were known to them. To their ears the only concordant intervals, or *melodic-relations*, were the fourth below and the fifth above a given note : and its octaves, above and below. The octave was divided into two *tetrachords* (or intervals of four notes) separated by a whole tone—that is, by the difference between the two consonant intervals. The tetrachord was, in its turn, sub-divided into three and only three, smaller intervals in three different ways, which were called by Aristides Quintilianus (B.C. 110), a disciple of Aristoxenus who seems to have been the first theorist to refer all questions of consonance and dissonance to the judgment of the ear rather than to that of mathematics, " the enharmonic, the chromatic, and the diatonic." " The diatonic," he says, " is so called because it proceeds by, or abounds in, *tones*, The chromatic is so termed because, as that which is between white and black is called Colour, so also that which holds the middle place between the two former genera as this does, is named Chroma. . . . The diatonic is the most natural of all, because it may be sung by everyone, even by such as are unlearned. The most artificial (τεχνικώτατον) is the chromatic, for only learned men can modulate it; but the most accurate is the enharmonic : it is approved of only by the most skilful musicians, for those who are otherwise look on the quarter-tone as an interval which can by no means be sung, and to these, by reason of the debility of their faculties, the use of this genus is impossible." Thus the diatonic tetrachord scale of the tonic A would run E, F, G, A; the chromatic, E, F, F sharp, A; and the enharmonic, E, the quarter-tone above E, F natural, A. It will be evident from the above that Greek music differed fundamentally from anything known in later European practice.[1]

Now, in spite of our old friend the Unko

---

[1] Intervals smaller than a semitone, and intervals compounded of semitones exceeded by such an interval may still be heard from folk-singers who have preserved the genuine tradition of folk-singing, particularly in the West of Ireland. For this reason there is a great disparity between Irish folk-songs as *heard* and the same songs as read from the printed page, as these intervals have never been measured accurately enough to permit of their being accurately notated. Cf. Béla Bartók : *Volksmusik der Rumänen von Maramures* (1923) on a similar phenomenon in the folk-music of Eastern Europe.

(*Hylobates   Rafflesii*) who has been heard by
travellers to sing complete chromatic scales with
perfect intonation and great intensity of feeling in the
forests and jungles of India, the diatonic genus
remained the most " natural " for human singers in
Europe, and by the eleventh century of the Christian
era, when Guido d'Arezzo devised his system of
Hexachords (or diatonic series of six notes with a semitonic interval between the third and fourth sounds), the
other two genera had been both in practice and theory
discarded in favour of it.   In Guido's system, which
consists of the simple transposition of the same series of
intervals on to different bases (Gamut, or the G on the
bottom line of the bass clef, C, F, G, c, f, g), we see
the root of the modern principles of scale and tonality.
The word *gamut* was used to signify both the lowest
note of the system and the entire scale of sounds contained in the system; and if we visualise the word
scale (which, of course, was never used in connection
with music until a much later date) literally as a
ladder, we shall find the different *modes* (or melodic
intervals considered in relation to compass) perched
upon its different rungs.[1]   But, to continue the figure
of speech, the rungs do not all occur at equal intervals.
For instance, between the third and fifth notes (A and
C) of the third hexachord (which begins on F) we find
not only the natural diatonic note of that hexachord
(B flat) intervening, but also the third note (B natural)
of the overlapping fourth hexachord which has begun

---

[1]   For the only lucid account of the modes in English, see R. O. Morris :
Contrapuntal Technique in the Sixteenth Century, which is the best book
on counterpoint in the English language, being based upon first-hand study
of the works of the great masters, not upon information gleaned from previous
theorists.

again on the G below. Sooner or later some relation-
ship will have to be established between them, although
at first sight they do not appear to be on speaking
terms.

We observe, however, that the passage from one
hexachord into the next above it is always made by
means of the semitonic interval: the principle
of the sharp " leading-note," apparently based upon
an instinctive demand of the ear coupled with a desire
to avoid the melodic interval of the tritone resulting
from a succession of three whole tones, is at once
apparent. The same principle necessitates the
flattening in *descent*, of the note which had been
sharpened in *ascent*. This sharpening and flattening
of the notes of a melody in accordance with the
dictates of the ear was known as *musica ficta*, music
made consequently false.

It will be readily seen that the combination of the
principle of *musica ficta* with that of transposition
could not but lead towards the filling up of the gaps
in the gamut and the establishment of what we now
regard as the complete chromatic scale. Long
before they recognized it as such, musicians
could contemplate the chromatic scale spread out
before their eyes on the keyboards of their organs and
virginals, and on the frets of their lutes. But we must
remember that as a matter of acoustical fact, G sharp
and A flat, for example, are far from being identical,
and it is only by the adoption of the compromising
system of equal temperament that we are enabled,
as a matter of convenience, to regard them as a single
note. They were, at any rate, clearly differentiated
in the minds of musicians for long after keyboard

instruments had come into common use. Thus
Thomas Morley in a certain passage in his *Plaine and
Easie Introduction to Practicall Musicke* (1597) says
" that those virginals which our unlearned musytians
cal cromatica (and some also grammatica) be not right
chromatica, but half enharmonica; and that al the
chromatica may be expressed uppon our common
virginals except this : [quoting the G-A flat above
middle C] for if you would thinke that the sharpe in
g sol re ut[1] would serve that turne by experiment, you
shall find that it is more than half a quarter of a note
too low." Yet less than twenty years after these
words were written, John Bull composed a piece for
the virginals in which these notes, A flat and G sharp,
both occur within the same bar. This goes far to
explain how Vincentino and other composers of the
same period " split upon enharmonic rocks and
chromatic quicksands "; and we can see how the term
enharmonic gradually lost its original meaning of a
quarter-tone, or smaller, interval and acquired its
present significance.

In attempting a rapid survey of the rise and
development of chromaticism during the three centuries preceding Gesualdo, it is necessary to make one
important reservation at the very outset. Our
evidence, for the earlier period, is almost exclusively
derived from the works of theorists who concerned
themselves almost exclusively with sacred music. The
eccleciastical authorities have always been averse to
experiments and innovations in the music of the
Church. It is therefore not surprising that from an age

---

[1] For a clear exposition of this method of nomenclature, see Grove's
Dictionary of Music and Musicians.   Article on *Solmization.*

when book learning and even the art of writing was largely confined to ecclesiastics the record that has survived of its musical achievements should be one-sided and therefore incomplete. The impulse to sing, from which the musically creative faculty arises, is a constant factor in the human mind, and the intuitions of creative minds have always necessarily preceded the theories which have been invented in the attempt to explain them in terms of verbal reason and logic. It is therefore extremely unlikely that anything more helpful to our æsthetic (as distinct from our archæological) appreciation of the music of the fifteenth and sixteenth centuries can be gleaned from the contemporary text-books, or the modern ones based upon them, than the very meagre assistance we obtain for our understanding of modern music from the academic treatises of the nineteenth century. There is no continuity in the history of musical theory. In sixteenth century music, particularly, one often comes across a passage which contemporary theorists would have been hard pressed to explain, yet such passages almost invariably have an air of complete assurance; there is nothing haphazard or tentative about them. The explanation is no doubt to be found in the absence of any adequate record of the secular music of the middle ages. We know that the Troubadours of the twelfth and thirteenth centuries developed the art of melodic composition to a very high degree of perfection, working along quite different lines from those pursued by the musicians of the Church. Giraldus Cambrensis, writing in the twelfth century, strikes a spark of light in the darkness in which the music of the people is enveloped in his account of the

improvised part-singing of Northumbria and Wales.
From the thirteenth century we have *Sumer is icumen
in*—another isolated beacon of light; and from the
fourteenth the astonishing songs of Guillaume de
Machault, which are in their way as audacious and
original as anything of Gesualdo.   There can be little
doubt that the influence of popular music on the work
of composers trained to the current theories of
composition became increasingly strong in the
fifteenth and sixteenth centuries, though we have little
direct evidence to corroborate the evidence provided
by these composers' own works.

Reverting to the early theorists, the thirteenth
century *Introductio musicae secundum Johannem de
Garlandia* tells us that " false music is when we make
a semitone of a tone," and conversely.   Every tone
is divisible into two semitones, and consequently signs
signifying semitones can be attached to all tones.[1]
Marchettus of Padua, writing in 1274, describes the
chromatic alteration of a note by means of accidentals
as *permutatio*, and quotes the following example :—

In a later work, dating from the early years of the
fourteenth century, Marchettus makes an interesting
protest against the term *musica falsa*.   The word false,
he argues, implies something that is bad or wrong, and
since accidentals are only introduced into music in

---

[1]   Falsa musica est quando de tono facimus semitonium et e converso.
Omnis tonus divisibilis est in duo semitonia et per consequens signa
semitonia designantia in omnibus tonis possunt amplificiari.

order to make it more harmonious and beautiful it would be better and more appropriate to call such music " coloured " (or as we should say, *chromatic*) and so avoid the suspicion that there was anything erroneous about it.[1] But by far the most important authority on mediæval chromaticism is Prosdocimus de Beldemandis whose *Tractatus de contrapunctu* dates from 1412. Prosdocimus tells us flatly that those who say that the whole tone can be divided into five equal parts are liars. He recognises only two kinds of semitone, calling the difference between them a " croma " (for example A flat—G sharp). Then, invoking the authority of his beloved and intellectually-enlightened colleague, Master Nicolaus de Collo de Conegliano, doctor of medicine and of the liberal arts, he says that there are two ways of dividing a tone into semitones, one by flattening the upper note, the other by sharpening the lower. By putting the two methods together, he arrives—the first theorist in musical history to do so—at a complete enharmonicchromatic scale of seventeen notes within the octave :

$$D^\flat C^\sharp \quad E^\flat D^\sharp \quad G^\flat F^\sharp \quad A^\flat G^\sharp \quad B^\flat A^\sharp$$
$$C \quad\quad D \quad\quad E\,F \quad\quad G \quad\quad A \quad\quad B$$

He admits that the notes D sharp and A sharp were very rarely used, but he shows where they may be found in case anyone should want them; and he gives a striking example of the use of accidentals in

---

[1] " Cum ergo tale signum sit repertum in musica ad pulcriores consonantias reperiendas et faciendas, et falsum in quantum falsum semper sumatur in mala parte potius quam in bona (quod est enim falsum, nunquam bonum est) : ideo salva reverentia aliorum dicimus, quod magis debet et proprius nominari musica colorata quam falsa, per quod nomen falsitatis [vituperium] attribuimus eidem."

counterpoint which seems all the more remarkable to us for its inclusion of the melodic interval of the tritone, or augmented fourth which earlier writers shunned as the devil and theorists long continued to prohibit.

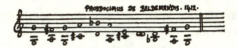

Thus Johannes Tinctoris, who was *maestro di cappella* at the court of Ferdinand of Aragon, King of Naples, from 1475 to 1487, and founded a school of music which was reorganized more than a century later by Gesualdo, says that augmented and diminished intervals should, if possible, be avoided, but admits that examples of their use can be found even in the works of the best masters.

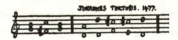

Despite the theoretical admission of the full range of chromaticism early in the fifteenth century, the licenses of *musica ficta* were very little used during the next hundred and fifty years. For a long while the use of accidentals was purely inflectional, occasioned by the line of individual voice parts for the sake of achieving smooth and easy cadences. If the employment of an accidental in one part caused a dissonance, such as an augmented or diminished interval, between that part and another, the harmonic effect was purely accidental and was originally regarded as a somewhat lamentable occurrence that could not be helped. The earlier composers aimed first at a good melodic line for each separate voice; then at rhythmic independence of parts. The vertical relation between one part and another, in unrhythmic note-against-note music, was confined to simple concords, save on the rare occasions when the use of an accidental in one part caused a momentary clash. The development of rhythmic independence of parts brought about the necessity for frequent suspensions or, as one might say, the overlapping of two chords, one voice anticipating or lagging behind the others. And now the word "chord" has perforce crept in as it should not at this early stage; for although the early contrapuntal composers obtained many beautiful effects of harmony and of tone-colour by careful spacing and grouping of their voices, they were always preoccupied with the horizontal aspect of their work, beauty of line in each part and what one may term the rhythmic *flow* of the whole piece. At a later date certain unusual combinations of sounds which had originally occurred *en passant*, as the result of interweaving two strands of rhythmically independent melody, were found to be good in themselves. These could be detached from their context and used elsewhere in a different way; and so we arrive at the idea of purely harmonic effects. It is, when you come to think of it, a miraculous thing that men who were entirely unaccustomed to think of music in terms of chords, yet managed to achieve (at first half unconsciously) by skilful manipulation of lines and rhythms alone harmonic effects of the greatest beauty and appropriateness. A passage like this, from a Mass of Brumel, composed in the early years of the sixteenth century,

strikes us as being as bold in its harmony as many a flight of the later chromaticists, yet it was certainly not thought of as harmony by the composer, all the fine effect being achieved by means of suspensions, passing notes and the rhythmic interplay of the different voice parts. We, who have all been brought up on the four-square tune harmonized in chords which are merely subsidiary to the tune, necessarily find it very difficult to cast our minds back to the time when music was conceived in terms of pure line. We find it hard to realize that a passage of Palestrina, for example, which seems to us to be a straightforward sequence of four-part chords, was undoubtedly conceived by the composer as four interwoven strands of melody. But if we fail to realize this fact, we cannot properly appreciate the significance of those composers who first thought of employing purely harmonic effects to heighten the expressive power of their music.

The madrigal—the most important form of secular music in the sixteenth century—came into being in Italy about the year 1530; and it is in the madrigals of the succeeding seventy-five years that the gradual development of the harmonic sense can best be studied. All through this period we find that the use of discords, chromaticism and bold original harmonic progressions, are invariably occasioned by some particular emotional point in the words of the madrigal which the composer wished to emphasize in his music. It is to the quest of ever more vivid means of expression rather than to any theoretical speculations that we owe the most important musical discoveries of the sixteenth century. As early as 1539 there occurs in a madrigal of Costanzo Festa a typical example of a method of emphasizing a particular word that persisted right through the century. Here the word *dolor* is illustrated by the use of a sudden discord :

About this time the influence of Adrian Willaert, a Flemish musician who had been appointed *maestro di cappella* of St. Mark's at Venice in 1527, began to make itself felt, though it is rather as an enlightened teacher, ever eager to encourage the researches and experiments of his pupils, than as a composer that the name of Willaert is remembered. His most distinguished pupil was Cipriano de Rore, who eventually succeeded him at St. Mark's; and it is on the title page of a book of madrigals by Cipriano that we first encounter, in any shape or form, the word *chromatic*—not curiously enough in the first edition, published in 1542, but in the second which appeared two years later under the title *Primo Libro de Madrigali Cromatici a cinque voci. Venetia, A. Gardano,* 1544. In the following year Vincenzo

Ruffo published a book of *Madrigali a quatro voci a notte negre* which, in the third edition (1552) are described as *Madrigali Cromatici*. Examples of the use of the word could be multiplied from the title-pages of madrigal books published about this time. The idea of a *new music* was in the air.   In 1546 appeared a volume entitled *Nicola Vicentino, del unico Adrian Willaerth discipulo . . Madrigali a cinque voci per Teorica et pratica da lui composti al nuovo modo dal celeberrimo suo maestro ritrovato.* In 1555 came *Orlando di Lasso's Quatorsiesme Livre à 4 parties* (18 *chansons italiennes*, 6 *chansons françaises*, 6 *Motets, à la Nouvelle composition d'aucuns d'Italie*) of which two editions were published by Tylman Susato at Antwerp, one in Italian and one in French.   And in 1559 Willaert issued a volume with the title *Musica Nova*.   Much of the " novelty " of the compositions contained in these books seems very tame to us when we compare it with what followed soon afterwards from Gesualdo and his contemporaries.   But even in this early period we find some very striking examples of adventurously chromatic harmony.   The following is from a madrigal, specially designated *Cromaticho*, by Cesare Tudino (1554):

It may be mentioned here, *à propos* the title of Tudino's book, that the word *cromatico* had at least two different meanings in the middle of the sixteenth century. One corresponded roughly to our present-day sense and implied semitonic inflections and the use of accidentals in the music; the other was derived from the fact that the Italian word for a crotchet (which was then considered a very short note, the use of which corresponded approximately to our modern use of the quaver) was, and still is, *croma*. In this sense the word *cromatico* implies the use of the crotchet instead of the customary minim as the unit of time in the composition. It is further possible that the word carried a double significance, for the crotchet was a black inky note and its satellite the quaver had a black inky tail, whereas the minim and the semibreve were white and open. The word *cromatico* might therefore convey the idea of *highly-coloured* figuration, notated in quavers and semiquavers which would impart to the printed page an appearance of singular and unwonted blackness.

The *Quatorsiesme Livre* of Orlando di Lasso referred to above contains two interesting specimens of chromatic writing in the two Latin odes "Alma Nemes" and "Calami sonum ferentes" set to music by Lasso and Cipriano de Rore respectively. (Both are printed in full in Burney's *General History of Music*). Of these Cipriano's is by far the most enterprising piece of work. Lasso, indeed, did but toy with the methods of the new school with which he doubtless became acquainted during his travels in Italy in the service of Ferdinand Gonzaza in the early fifteen-fifties. He was certainly in Rome in June, 1551, when Vicentino and Lusitano held their famous public debate on the question of the three " genera "

—diatonic, chromatic and enharmonic—and being at that time a young man he may have been somewhat impressed by the expressive possibilities offered by the new theories. But he seems to have become dissatisfied with the new methods in later life, employing chromaticism only to express such words as *error*, *distortion* and *evil* in his texts. The closing bars of his Latin ode may be quoted here :

Cipriano de Rore appears to have been a composer of very considerable attainments, but practically nothing of his work has been reprinted in modern times. His Latin ode displays not only an harmonic sense very much in advance of that of his contemporaries, but also a remarkable sense of tone--colour, being designed for the unusual combination of four bass voices which would impart a singular atmosphere of gloom to the close chromatic harmonies. It is possible that an even earlier date than 1555 may be assigned to this astonishing composition. Lasso would seem to have included it in his book as an act of homage to the elder master, and as a kind of acknowledgment to the work on which he had modelled his own composition on similar lines, which shows that Rore's ode was presumably well-known when Lasso was in Italy. The opening bars of the ode may be quoted here :

together with a curiously Tannhäuserish passage from
the middle of the work :

Another beautiful example of Cipriano's use of
novel harmonic progressions, combined with a fine
feeling for phrase and cadence occurs in the madrigal
" Dalle belle contrade," from the fifth book of five-
part madrigals (1566) :

The year 1555 is also notable for the publication
of Vicentino's treatise *L'antica Musica ridotta alla*

moderna prattica in which the author expounds at great length his theories of the three " genera " and also describes his " Archicembalo," a keyboard instrument with six manuals, so tuned that every tone was divided into five parts; and in 1558 appeared the famous *Istitutioni armonishe* of Zarlino which contains an account of a quarter-tone keyboard instrument which Zarlino had built ten years earlier. Nor were these by any means the only experiments made at this period with the object of enlarging the potential range of musical sounds.

It cannot be said that Vicentino displayed any great talent or originality as a composer, in spite of his description of himself, on the title-page of his fifth book of five-part madrigals published in 1572 as *l'arcimusico . . . Pratico et theorico et inventore delle nuove harmonie.* But he was certainly a bold adventurous spirit who probably exerted a very considerable influence upon the composers of his day.

Brief mention of the *Madrigali Cromatici* of Giandomenico La Martoretta (1552), Vincenzo Ruffo (1552), Giulio Fiesco (1554), Pietro Taglia (1555), Francesco Manara (1555) and Francesco Orso (1567), whose setting of the 164th Sonnet of Petrarch shows a very considerable degree of skill and imagination in the illustrative treatment of words, and Ludovico Agostini (1570), will suffice to show how widespread was the chromatic movement at this time. Even Palestrina was not wholly unaffected by it.[1] All through this period we see the gradual breaking-up of

---

[1] See Peter Wagner : *Das Madrigal und Palestrina* : Vierteljahrschrift für Musikwissenschaft 1892, VIII, where a large number of references to Palestrina's work are given.

the old modal system by the growing forces of chromaticism. The Guidonian hexachord which had hitherto provided the basis of all musical instruction was challenged by several speculative theorists, notably by Hubert Waelrant of Antwerp (1517-1595) who added a seventh syllable to the six in ordinary use, thus giving a clearer definition to the principle of the leading-note. The old conception of *enharmonic* as implying the use of quarter-tones gradually gave way to the modern sense—by 1581 we find Marenzio's employing the notes F sharp and G flat in the same chord. Notation, too, passed through certain experimental phases of which the most curious was Orso's method of notating a rising chromatic sequence of notes, writing

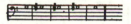

where the effect intended was

The most common method of noting chromatic alterations was by the placing of an accidental immediately before each note which was to be raised or lowered. This method, having first been employed in unbarred music was continued without modification for some time after the introduction of lute tablature and vocal music in score had rendered the use of bars almost essential. In sixteenth and early seventeenth century music, as a general rule, all notes are *naturals* except those immediately preceded by an accidental.

There was no specific sign for a *natural*, although
sometimes we find a sharpened note specifically made
natural by the use of the ♭ sign, or a flattened note
specifically naturalized by a ♯. If, however, an F♯
occurred on the first beat of a bar, the ♯ would not
necessarily affect any subsequent F which might occur
within that bar; without further evidence to the
contrary the second F must be assumed to be natural.

Experiments in "word-painting," of considerable
interest from the technical point of view, and by no
means negligible from the æsthetic, were made by
Rocco Rodio[1] (1587) and Giuseppe Caimo (1585).
Here is a remarkable example of Caimo's treatment of
the words " aspre spine " (sharp thorns):

But all these composers fade into comparative
insignificance beside the distinguished figure of Luca
Marenzio, the greatest of all the Italian madrigalists.
In melodic invention, allied to the most consummate
skill in the handling of polyphonic structures in the
traditional manner, he was rivalled only by Palestrina
among his own countrymen; but while Palestrina paid
but little heed to the methods of the newer harmonic
school, Marenzio, like his great English peer and
contemporary, William Byrd, was keenly alive to
the possibilities of the new style. While the

---

[1] A theorist as well as a composer, whose *Regole per far contrappunto
sole e accompagnato nel canto fermo* (1600) was reprinted in 1609 and again
in 1626.

composers of his day were playing somewhat crudely with the new devices, the genius of Marenzio enabled him to master them completely and to assimilate them into the contrapuntal technique of tradition.   Thus while sacrificing none of the older polyphonic methods he was able to enrich them with the added wealth of chromaticism and the new harmonic resources derived from it.   In the following extract from Marenzio's 9th book of five-part madrigals (1599) one hardly knows whether to admire most the bold melodic outlines and independence of the individual parts, the strikingly original progressions of harmony, or the magnificent shape and structure of the whole passage which illustrates with such perfection the spirit of the words which inspired it :

Solo e pensoso i piu deserti campi
Vo' misurando a passi tarde lento.[1]

---

[1] Alone and pensive I wandered with slow and measured steps through the deserted fields.

It is but reasonable to suppose that the work of Marenzio exercised a considerable influence upon the English school of madrigalists which flourished, roughly, between the year of the Spanish Armada and accession of King Charles the First. The fact that a number of Marenzio's madrigals were published in this country with English words in Nicholas Yonge's *Musica Transalpina* (1588) and Thomas Watson's *Italian Madrigals Englished* (1590) seems to show that these works had already attained a certain popularity here in their original form. But Marenzio's influence was rather in the direction of solid polyphonic technique than in that of harmonic innovations. It is true that as early as 1588 William Byrd warned the reader of his *Psalms, Sonnets, and Songs* that " In the expressing of these songs, either by voyces or Instruments, if ther happen to be any jarre or dissonance, blame not the Printer who (I doe assure thee) through his great paines and diligence doth heere deliver to thee a perfect and true Coppie "; and within the ordinary modal limits the English composers of the latter half of the sixteenth century are perhaps rather freer in their harmony than their Italian contemporaries of the Roman School. But it is not until the last three years of the century that we encounter real chromaticism in English music, and then it appears in so astonishingly mature a form and is handled in such a masterly manner that it is evident that the principles underlying it had been thoroughly implanted in our composers for some considerable time. The following extract from a Canzonet by Giles Farnaby (1598), a composer chiefly famous for his bold and original compositions for keyboard

instruments, may well be compared with Marenzio's *Solo e pensoso*, though, as the dates of publication show, there is no question of its being in any way derivative.

The English school provides other superb examples of the expressive use of chromaticism in Thomas Weelkes's three-part madrigal *Cease sorrows now* (1597), and his six-part *O care, thou wilt despatch me* (1600), in John Dowland's ayre *I saw my lady weep* (1600), and above all in John Danyel's wonderful setting (1606) of the words :

> Can doleful notes to measured accents set
> Express unmeasured griefs which time forget?
> No, let chromatic tunes, harsh without ground,
> Be sullen music for a tuneless heard.

The employment of chromatic harmony, both in England and in Italy, was nearly always prompted by the idea of pain or doubt, though in certain madrigals it is associated with the *dolcezza amare* of lovers, and so acquires a character of almost excessive sweetness —which it has retained to this day.

III

When all acknowledgment has been duly paid to the work of his predecessors in the field of harmonic expressionism, Gesualdo stands out in isolation as a figure of extraordinary originality and indubitable genius. It is perhaps only when his work is exhibited side by side with specimens of the earlier harmonists that its unique quality can be appreciated at its true value. His influence on his contemporaries and on the generation which succeeded him is more difficult to estimate. Contemporary evidence would persuade us that it was considerable, but the study of seventeenth century harmony is greatly complicated by the fact that in the early years of the century it became customary to publish only the principal melody of a work together with a figured bass which it was left to the performer to fill up, on the lute, organ or harpsichord, at his own discretion. Many of the accompanied solo songs of the first half of the century contain harmonies which, on the bare evidence of their figured basses, are in the highest degree fantastic and experimental; and it may safely be said that, did we not possess the works of Gesualdo, we should be completely at a loss to explain the reason for so sudden and widespread a movement in the direction of harmonic liberty. The mere appearance of the figured bass in the publications of the period argues a very considerable acquaintance with the principles of harmony, conceived as such, on the part of the musical public. This, of course, is very largely to be attributed to the development and increasing use of

keyboard instruments; but the work of Gesualdo which, as we have seen, achieved a quite extraordinary degree of notoriety, was without doubt very largely responsible for the sudden expansion of the range of harmony itself.

Harmony, as Delius, its greatest modern master, has repeatedly said, is an instinct. Either you are born with it, or else you have to do without it. The same thing may be said of the gift of melodic invention. On the other hand, counterpoint—in so far as one can detach counterpoint from the ability to invent melodies and combine them in orderly and harmonious relation—can be learned and acquired by study. Nothing is easier than to compose an indifferent madrigal or fugue if you follow closely enough the rules and examples of the text-book without a thought for original invention or musical beauty. It is therefore manifestly absurd to suppose that Gesualdo wrote as he did because he could not sufficiently master the ordinary principles of contrapuntal composition. Many of his early madrigals are dull enough, to our ears, as music, but their very dullness is individual; it is not as other men's dullness —and there is, in all conscience, a liberal enough supply of dull music from this period to compare it with. From the very outset we can see that Gesualdo, like Berlioz, Moussorgsky, Delius and many another instinctive composer, was always occupied with the problem of personal expression. As a matter of fact he had at his disposal a very good equipment of contrapuntal technique of the traditional kind—as witness the two madrigals from the first book, *Felice Primavera* and *Danzan le Ninfe*, which have been reprinted by Mr. Barclay Squire. Even in his most mature and, harmonically, most advanced compositions the line of an individual voice part generally shows us quite logically how the most surprising progression has been brought about; a single note in one of the parts, chromatically altered by an accidental, becomes a kind of pivot on which the harmony swings away from the expected resolution into what in modern parlance would be called a remote key. His boldest flights of imagination impress one by the mastery with which they are introduced in the course of a composition so traditional in form and so essentially polyphonic in conception as the madrigal. Every note tells, every strange modulation has its particular, its precise significance. Having all the old polyphonic technique at his disposal, he grafted on to it, so to speak, his own very individual harmonic resources and so blended the two styles that there is never any feeling of incongruity between them; they have become one and indivisible. These madrigals show that the so-called homophonic revolution which is supposed to have dethroned polyphony at the end of the sixteenth century is a mere figment of the historians' imagination. Gesualdo was always a polyphonist in his methods, yet there are harmonic passages in his work to which we should not find parallels until we come to Wagner. If anyone doubts this statement, let him compare the opening of Gesualdo's *Moro lasso al mio duolo*, from the sixth book, with the famous chord-sequence in *Die Walküre* which is heard when Wotan kisses Brünnhilde to sleep, and—a nearer parallel seeing that it occurs in a work for unaccompanied chorus—with the chord-

sequence to which the words " sound of the water "
are set in Delius's *On Craig Dhu* :

Things of this kind must certainly have seemed
crude and tentative, fantastic almost to the point of
insanity, to the historians of the eighteenth and nineteenth centuries. It is true that there were a few who
appreciated them, but they were isolated exceptions.
In the light of the musical developments of the last
five-and-twenty years, however, we see them not as
stammering and experimental utterances in a new
idiom but as miracles of perfected craft and

expression, not as the beginning of a new era of music —for they stand in complete isolation, almost without ancestry, completely without successors—but as one of the crowning glories of the old order of polyphony. Modern music is teaching us reverence for the old masters.   We no longer dare to " correct " their works, to alter them and titivate them in a futile endeavour to make them conform to the conventions of an age other than their own, for we no longer wish to do so.   We can see beauty and a perfect sense of fitness in dissonances which to our predecessors seemed meaningless and were treated as miscalculations or misprints; and we can see that the best of the old music is as vital to-day as it was when it was written, in spite of its having been relegate to the dusty shelves of libraries for over two centuries.   It speaks to us with a living voice in a language which, whatever changes of idiom may be imposed by passing time, is changeless and eternal and can never fail to evoke a response in the hearts of all who have ears and will hear.

The most cursory examination of the Molinaro score is sufficient to give the lie to Burney's charge of technical incompetence, about which Fetis says, with considerable penetration : " Ce jugement, aussi sévère qu'injuste, prouve seulement que Burney n'a pas compris la pensée originale qui domine dans les madrigaux du prince de Venouse.   Tous ces morceaux sont des scènes mélancoliques et douces, où le musicien s'est proposé d'exprimer le sens poétique des paroles, suivant sa manière individuelle de sentir. . . . Le système de succession des tons employé par Gesualdo n'est pas la modulation véritable car l'élément harmonique de l'enchaînement des tonalités n'existait pas encore lorsqu'il écrivait, mais ces successions mêmes sont une partie de sa pensée et Burney avait tort de les juger d'après les règles ordinaires."

Gesualdo was reaching out not towards tonality, in the academic sense of the word, but beyond it. At his best he is very much nearer to the modern composer who sets in juxtaposition, at the dictates of his inner ear, chords which are theoretically unrelated. He had no idea of establishing a definite tonality in his works, and no more desire to be bound by the key-system than by the modal system. But it was certainly not any lack of ability that made him choose this path. If he had wished to write conventional diatonic harmony, he had all the necessary technique to do so—and more : witness the extraordinary certainty of some of his sequential modulations—as, for instance, his treatment of the words "d'amor empia homicida" in the madrigal *Tu m'uccidi o crudele*.

He is a perfect master of the short, poignant phrase—precursor of the *leit-motif*—whether it be an expressive melodic fall or a striking harmonic progression, or a combination of the two. Examples are plentiful throughout his work. Already in the second book (which as we have seen is actually the first) our attention is arrested by his profoundly moving treatment of the words, " O come e gran martire "—words which Monteverdi had set, two years previously with far less telling effect. Look at the sombrely impressive opening of *Sparge la morte* in Book IV, the expressive downward leap of a seventh in the six-part *Donna se m'ancidete* at the end of the third book (an effect repeated with added emphasis in *Cor mio deh non piangete* (Book IV), the plaintive questioning phrase *Tu piangi ò Filli mia?* (Book VI), above all the noble beginning of *Moro lasso* which, though it disgusted the ear of Dr. Burney, drew a panegyric from Winterfeld and seemed to Kroyer "an ideal embodiment of majestic sorrow." Look at the enigmatic close of *Mille volte il di moro*, with its melodic fall of a diminished fifth on to the final chord. How remarkable his endings are! The voices fade mysteriously into silence, and yet how cunningly—for all its unconventionality—is the final cadence contrived, how firmly the texture of the music is held together by a sustained pedal note in the highest or lowest voice—sometimes in both.[1] Look at his impassioned exclamations—*cris de cœur* which seem to be left suspended in the air, while other voices gravely comment or continue the plaint (there is masterly use of the different registers of the voices in varied effects of tone-colour to be observed here).

But it is not fair to Gesualdo's craftsmanship to represent him only by short excerpts. I have therefore given, in the appendix, two complete madrigals, in order to show how skilfully he can weld together a number of short phrases and sequences into a rhythmically balanced whole. Their form and line is more broken than that of the best English madrigals

---

[1] It is an interesting point that among all his harmonic experiments Gesualdo never attempted a full close on a minor chord. To sharpen the third of the final chord, or else omit altogether, was merely an idiomatic convention of the time, so we must not read any deliberate attempt to surprise into Gesualdo's sudden transitions from minor to major at the end of a madrigal.

which, heard or read, pass through the mind in majesty like galleons in full sail; but these two specimens of Gesualdo's art are none the less consummate achievements of musical expression.

Moussorgsky himself was not more careful to make his music the exact equivalent of the word than were some of the madrigalists of the end of the sixteenth century. Examples may be found of words like *respiro, soletto, misero,* characterised by being set to the notes *re, sol,* and *mi* of the Guidonian hexachord; this, of course, was a mere piece of pedantic extravagance. But in the more legitimate and æsthetically effective devices of word-painting the masters of this period attained to as high a degree of proficiency as has even been reached in subsequent centuries. It was often overdone, to such an extent that the musical thought became entirely subservient to the business of making verbal points. Thus in the preface of Philip Rosseter's *Book of Airs* (1601) we find the author (probably Campion) remarking : " But there are some who, to appeare the more deepe and singular in their judgment, will admit no Musicke but that which is long, intricate, bated with fuge, chaind with syncopation, and where the nature of everie word is precisely exprest in the Note, like the old exploided action in Comedies, when if they did pronounce *Memeni,* they would point to the hinder part of their heads, if *Video,* put their finger in their eye. But such childish observing of words is altogether ridiculous, and we ought to maintaine as well in Notes as in action a manly cariage, gracing no word, but that which is eminent and emphaticall."

It has been suggested that Gesualdo was the first

of the long line of musicians who have " composed at
the piano " (or whatever keyboard instrument
happened to be handy at the time), a suggestion which
is supported by the indisputable fact that before the
middle of the sixteenth century, harmony was indeed
regarded as a secondary, almost automatic product of
concurrent streams of melody.   There is not the
slightest doubt that keyboard instruments helped to
bring about in men's minds a definite conception of
chords as chords—and more particularly of discords
(in the technical sense of chords requiring resolution)
as such in isolation and not merely heard in passing,
by way of suspensions, etc.   But it is one thing to
fumble about on the piano in the hope of making a
discovery of the kind celebrated in "The Lost
Chord," and a very different matter to turn that
discovery to significant account in a composition. We
never find in Gesualdo's work such things as
sequences of chords moving about in semitones in
similar motion or any of the obvious and almost
inevitable discoveries of the keyboard-fumbler. Every
progression of chords in his work seems to be the
result of clear and definite musical thought.

The form of Gesualdo's madrigals is almost
invariably conditioned by verbal antitheses.   The
harmonic and contrapuntal styles seem to have been
sharply differentiated in his mind, quite apart from
any consideration of the notes—combinations or
figurations—employed in either; he pits the one style
against the other in different sections of a madrigal
according as the sentiment of the text (which is always
stated, emphasized even, by a kind of key-word,
never merely suggested) provides him with oppor-

tunities of sudden change. Slow, strange progressions
of chords and short, heart-rending cries of melody are
reserved for the expression of grief, suffering and
thoughts of death; brilliant contrapuntal writing,
generally in rapid groups of semiquavers, with no
special melodic or harmonic significance, will always
accompany the words *joy, movement, ardour*, etc. He
seems to have so concentrated his peculiar genius upon
the expression of doleful sentiments that his joyful
moods are apt to appear perfunctory and almost
negative by contrast : and it is interesting in this
connection to compare him with some of the
protagonists of the nineteenth century Romantic
movement. In both we see the same preoccupation
with the darker aspects of life, the tragic, the grisly
and the bizarre. The high-lights and shadows are
perhaps exaggerated at times, but a fine proportion
and a sort of formal balance of opposing sections is
always maintained. Where Gesualdo falls short
(he can hardly be said to fail in what he never seems
to attempt) is in sustained melody.[1] Weelkes's
madrigal *Hence, Care, thou art too cruel*, is as
antithetical and full of word-painting as any
of Gesualdo's : but the Prince could never have
written the lovely, smooth-flowing passage to which
Weelkes has set the words " Come Music, sick man's
jewel." He lacks the serenity and the reflective dignity
of the best English masters, in comparison with whom
he seems, to an English mind at any rate, almost

---

[1] This lends additional absurdity to the suggestion of Tassoni (1646)
that he was influenced by the compositions (now lost, if indeed they ever
existed) of James I, King of Scotland—a statement which gave rise to the
further supposition that traces of " Scottish melodies " could be found in
Gesualdo's madrigals !

sensational.   His art is turbulent, passionate, based
upon violent contrasts and sudden variations of mood
and, if Anatole France's sketch of him be founded on
fact, " c'était un seigneur très redouté pour son
humeur jalouse et violente.   Ses ennemis lui
reprochaient sa ruse et sa cruauté.   Ils l'appelaient
mâtin de renard et de louve et deux fois bête puante."
Such a temperament is by no means incompatible with
the tenderness and elegaic suavity his music so often
exhibits.   But we must beware of reading auto-
biography into his works as Keiner does when he
suggests that Gesualdo turned to music as a consola-
tion after the death of his first wife, and that the mood
of melancholy which pervades the greater part of his
work was the direct outcome of that tragic circum-
stance.   Gesualdo was a pure creative artist and the
prevailing mood of his music was conditioned by his
temperament, not by external events.

For all his pictorialism he was a very " absolute "
musician who generally expressed in his music a far
profounder thought than that of the poem he was
ostensibly setting.   He could concentrate his whole
idea of mortality into a madrigal apparently concerned
with no more tragic contingency than the unkindness
of a fair lady and the euphemistic " death " that would
results from her persistence in so hard-hearted a mood;
and the texts of some of his very finest madrigals are
such miserable specimens of poetry—sometimes they
remind   one   very   forcibly   of   the   present-day
" ballad "—that one can only feel that he regarded
his texts for the most part merely as framework for his
music.   His insistence on the word was in reality
not literalism at all, but a kind of universalisation, a

distilling of the quintessence of the word itself quite apart from its particular context and significance in the poem in question; and we find that the words he is most often inspired by are just those which in themselves have a universal emotional import—*sospiri, dolore, martire, morte* . . . and so on.

In short, Gesualdo was a composer of extraordinary genius whose works, for all the oblivion into which they have fallen, still live, in the fullest sense of the word, as the vivid and passionate expression of a strange personality. While Peri and Monteverdi were bringing to birth that new vehicle of expression which was to become the opera, Gesualdo, without the aid of action and a theatre, was dramatising the emotions themselves—and his contribution to the first period of dramatic music was no less important than theirs. Historical preoccupations are often apt to blind one to the purely æsthetic significance of works of art. The great monuments of sculpture and architecture need no elucidation or commentary; we have the works themselves and what they do not reveal to the mind that contemplates them can never be discovered by reading and research. But when we come to old music, we have not got the music itself, but only a symbol of it, whose accuracy, or rather whose all-sufficiency, we cannot help doubting at times (there are, of course, no indications of tempo, dynamics or expression in sixteenth and early seventeenth century music).

Perhaps some day the music itself will come back to us. The most fantastic imaginings of one century are wont to become the merest commonplaces of the next. Imagine the scornful contempt with which an Elizabethan would have greeted the man who told him that, latent among mankind's potentialities, lay the power to fly through the air, the power to capture the sound of a man's voice and reproduce it years after his death, the power to sing into a little box in America and be heard in London.   Yet all these things have come to pass; and I for one look forward hopefully to the time when—since no sound uttered in this world is ever wholly lost—some scientific method will be devised for disentangling the innumerable sound-waves of the centuries and tracing them back to their several sources; or some faculty of clairaudience be discovered which will save the memory of neglected genius from its present unhappy dependence upon the activities of insufficiently enthusiastic archæologists on the one hand, and insufficiently informed enthusiasts on the other.

BIBLIOGRAPHICAL APPENDIX

(1) The Works of Gesualdo as Originally Published

1594. Five-part Madrigals. Book 1, printed in Ferrara by Vittorio Baldini, the ducal printer, with a dedicatory preface by Scipione Stella, dated May 10th, 1594. Reprinted in 1603, 1607, 1616 (by Angelo Gardano, Venice).

Contents

Caro amoroso neo	O mio soave ardore
Ma se tale hà costei	Sento che nel partire
Se per lieve ferita	Non e questa la mano
Hai rotto, e sciolto	Ne tien face, ò saetta
Che sentir deve	Candida man
In più leggiadro velo	Da l'odorate spoglie
Se cosi dolce è il duolo	E quella Arpa felice
Ma se avverra ch'io moia	Non mai non cangierò
Se taccio il duol s'avvanz	All' apparir di quelle
O come è gran martire	Non mi toglia il ben mio

1594. Five-part Madrigals. Book 2, printed in Ferrara by Vittorio Baldini, the ducal printer, with a dedicatory preface by Scipione Stella, dated June 2nd, 1594. Reprinted 1603 (Venice), 1604 (Naples), 1607 and 1616 (Venice), 1617 (Naples).

Contents

Baci soavi e cari	O dolce mio martire
Quanto hà di dolce Amore	Tirsi morir volea
Madonna io ben vorrei	Frenò Tirsi il desio
Come esser può	Mentre mia stella miri
Gelo hà Madonna il seno	Non mirare non mirare
Mentre Madonna	Questi leggiadri
Ahi troppo saggia	Felice Primavera
Se da si nobil mano	Danzan le Ninfe
Amor pace non chero	Son si belle le rose
Si gioioso mi fanno	Bell' Angioletta

131

1595. Five-part Madrigals. Book 3, printed in Ferrara by Vittorio Baldini, the ducal printer, with a dedicatory preface by Hettore Gesualdo, dated March 19th, 1595. Reprinted in Venice 1603, 1611, and 1619.

Contents

Voi volete ch'io mora	Non t'amo ò voce ingrata
Moro ò non moro	Meraviglia d'amore
Ahi disperata vita	Et ardo e vivo
Languisco e moro	Crudelissima doglia
Del bel de bei vostri occhi	Se piange ohime
Ahi dispietata e cruda	Ancidetemi pur
Dolce spirto d'amore	Se vi miro pietosa
Sospirava il mio core	Deh se già fu crudele
O mal nati messaggi	Dolcissimo sospiro
Veggio sì dal mio sole	Donna se m'ancidete
	(six-part)

1596. Five-part Madrigals. Book 4, printed in Ferrara by Vittorio Baldini, the ducal printer, with a dedicatory preface by Hettore Gesualdo without date. Reprinted 1604, 1611, and 1616 (Venice).

Contents

Luci serene, e chiare	Sparge la morte al mio
Tal'hor sano desio	Moro, e mentre sospiro
Io tacerò ma nel silentio	Quando di lui la sospirata
In van dunque ò crudele	Mentre mira colei
Che fai meco mio cor	A voi mentre il mio core
Questa crudele, e pia	Ecco morirò dunque
Hor che in giora	Ahi già mi discoloro
O sempre crudo Amore	Arde il mio cor
Cor mio deh non piange	Se chiudete nel core
Dunque non m'offendete	Il sol qual hor più (six-part)
Volgi mia luce (six-part)	

1603. Sacrae Cantiones Book 1, for five voices. Printed in Naples by Constantino Vitali and published by Don Giovanni Pietro Cappuccio.

1603. Sacrae Cantiones Book 1, for six and seven voices. Published and printed as above.

1611. Responsoria. For six voices. Printed in Naples by Giovanni Jacomo Carlino. The only known copies of these three books of sacred music are in the library of the "Oratorio dei Filippini," at Naples. The present writer has not been able to examine them.

1611. Five-part Madrigals. Book 5, printed in Gesualdo by Giovanni Jacomo Carlino with a dedicatory preface by Don Giovanni Pietro Cappuccio, dated 20th June, 1611. Reprinted in 1614 in Venice by Bartholomeo Magni il Gardano, who adds a new dedication to Alfonso Strozzi, dated January 1st, 1614, with his "best wishes for the New Year."

Contents

Gioite voi col canto	Mercè grido piangendo
S'io non miro non moro	O voi troppo felici
Itene ò miei sospiri	Correte amanti à prova
Dolcissima mia vita	Asciugate i begli occhi
O dolorosa gioia	Tu m'uccidi ò crudele
Qual fora donna	Deh coprite il ben seno
Felicissimo sonno	Poi che l'avida sete
Se vi duole il mio duolo	Ma tu cagion di quella
Occhi del mio cor vita	O tenebroso giorno
Languisco al sin	Se tu fuggi io non resto

T'amo mia vita.

1611. Five-part Madrigals. Book 6, printed in Gesualdo by Giovanni Jacomo Carlino, with a dedicatory preface by Don Giovanni Pietro Cappuccio, dated 15th July, 1611. Reprinted in Venice, 1616.

Contents

Se la mia morte brami	Candido e verde fiore
Beltà poi che t'assenti	Ardita Zanzaretta
Resta di darmi noia	Ardo per te mio bene
Tu piangi ò Filli mia	Ancide sol la morte
Chiaro risplender suole	Quel nò crudel
Io parto e non più dissi	Moro lasso al mio duolo
Mille volte il dì moro	Volan quasi farfalle
O dolce mio tesoro	Al mio gioir il ciel si fa sereno
Deh come in van sospiro	Tu segui ò bella Clori
Io pur respiro	Ancor che per amarti
Alme d'amor rubelle	Già piansi nel dolore

Quando ridente e bella

1613. Score of the six books of five-part madrigals. Printed in Genoa by Giuseppe Pavoni and published by Simone Molinaro, *Maestro di Cappella* of the Cathedral of Genoa.

1626 (posthumous).   Six-part Madrigals, printed in Naples by
  Ambrosio Magnetta and published by Mutio Effrem
  with a dedicatory preface to the Prince's widow,
  Donna Leonora d'Èste-Gesualdo, dated 15th July,
  1626.   Of this work one voice part alone (the Quinto)
  survives, in the Library of the Liceo Musicale,
  Bologna.

Contents

Quale spada	L'arco amoroso
Parlo misero	Sfogando (in 2 sections)
Tu che non	Frà chare danze
Dove fuggi mio	Videla poi
Sei disposto (in 2 sections)	De bei colori
Pietà signore	Perche tal
Cor mio benche	Hai come
Non è questa	Gravid 'il
O chiome	Quando vaga

Two short madrigals (which are rather in the nature of
Canzonetti, having several verses to the same music), were
printed at the end of Pomponio Nenna's eighth book of
madrigals (1618).   These do not appear in any other volume.

Three madrigals from Gesualdo's second book reappear in
Scipione Stella's *Nuova Scelta di Madrigali di sette autori*
(Naples, 1615), Nenna and Dentice being included among the
seven composers.

---

(2)   REFERENCES TO GESUALDO BY HIS
CONTEMPORARIES.

1585.   Giovanni Leon Primavera dedicates his 7th book of five-
  part madrigals to Gesualdo.

1594.   Luzzasco Luzzaschi dedicates his 4th book of madrigals
  to Don Carlo Giesoaldi (*sic.*) in Ferrara.

1595.   Sebastian Raval, "Gentilhuomo Spagnuolo dell'
  Ordine di S. Giovanni Battista Hierosolimitano,"
  dedicates two madrigals in his *Madrigali a tre voci*
  (published in Rome to Gesualdo: "Con alcun

studio, non già certo, che arrivino di gran lunga alla composition di si gran Principe al colmo d'ogni perfettione, l'ho raccolti, e gli mando in luce composti per soggetti tali, gli dedico a V.S. . . .''

1615. D. Romano Micheli, in his *Musica Vaga et artificiosa,* gives an interesting list of musicians living in Naples in the time of Gesualdo : "In Napoli essendo io al servitio dell' Illustrissimo et Eccellentissimo Sig. Prencipe di Venosa con li Signori Musici Scipione Stella, Gio. Battista di Pavola, Mutio Effrem, e Pomponio Nenna, in tempo che erano li Signori Bartolomeo Roi Maestro di Cappella, e Gio. Macque Organista nella Cappella del Vice Re, viventi Rocco Rodio, Scipione Cerretto, Giustiniano Forcella, e Domenico Montella, musici peritissmi.''

References to Gesualdo also occur in the following books :

1601. Cerreto, Scipione, "Della prattica Musica vocale et strumentale.''

1615. Blancanus, Josephus, "Chronologia celebrorum Mathematicorum ad sec. Christi XVII.''

1613. Cerone, Pietro, "El Melopeo y Maestro.''

1622. Peacham, Henry, " The Compleat Gentleman.''

1635. Doni, Giov. Batt., collected works.

1636. Mersenne, M., "Harmonie Universelle.''

1650. Kircher, Athanasius, " Musurgia Universalis.''

1650. Vossius, Gerhard, "De Universae matheseos natura et constitutione.''

1706. Spagna, Archangelo, "Oratorii overo Melodrammi.''

---

(3) MODERN REPRINTS OF GESUALDO'S WORKS.

(A) *In a form convenient for the use of singers.*

(a) Four volumes devoted to Gesualdo in the *Raccolta Nazionale delle Musiche Italiane,* published in 1919 by the Instituto

Editoriale Italiano in Milan, under the editorship of Ildebrando Pizzetti, contain :

O come è gran martire	*From Book I*
Baci soavi e cari	*From Book II*
Quanto ha di dolce Amore	,, ,,
Tirsi morir volea	,, ,,
Freno Tirsi il desio	,, ,,
Languisco e moro	*From Book III*
Non t'amo ò voce ingrata	,, ,,
Meraviglia d'Amore	,, ,,
Io tacero	*From Book IV*
Sparge la morte	,, ,,
Arde il mio cor	,, ,,
O dolorosa gioia	*From Book V*
Merce grido piangendo	,, ,,
Tu m'uccidi ò crudele	,, ,,
Resta di darmi noia	*From Book VI*
Volan quasi farfalle	,, ,,

The reader is cautioned against two misprints which occur in this edition of *Tu m'uccidi* (Quaderno 62, page 11). The last note on the page for the first voice should be D, not C; and the corresponding note in the third voice should be B, not A.

(*b*) Breitkopf and Härtel publish in their series *Ausgewählte Madrigale,* edited by W. Barclay Squire :

Felice Primavera	
Danzan le Ninfe	*From Book II*

(*c*) Joseph Williams, Ltd., publish, under the editorship of J. B. McEwen :

Resta di darmi noia	
Moro lasso	*From Book VI*

The Italian texts are not given in this edition, and the English versions are excessively bad, causing phrases to be broken up, accents to be misplaced, and the significance of the striking harmonic progressions which Gesualdo uses to express particular words such as *dolorosa, morte,* etc., to be entirely lost.

(B) Madrigals reprinted in collections or books.

Luigi Torchi : *L'Arte Musicale in Italia,* Vol. IV, prints

Non t'amo ò voce ingrata
Donna se m'ancidete
Itene ò miei sospiri
Dolcissima mia vita
Già piansi nel dolore

Kiesewetter : *Schicksale und Beschaffenheit des weltlichen Gesanges* (1841)

Moro e mentre sospiro

Prince de la Moskowa : *Receuil des morceaux de musique ancienne*

Come esser puo
Gelo ha Madonna il seno

Martini : *Saggio di Contrappunto* (1774)

Donna se m'ancidete
Freno Tirsi il desio
Moro e mentre sospiro

Hawkins : *History of Music* (1776)

Baci soavi e cari
Quanto ha di dolce Amore

Burney : *A General History of Music* (1776)

Moro lasso

Ambros : *Geschichte der Musik*

Resta di darmi noia

Keiner : *Die Madrigale Gesualdos*

Mercè grido

Riemann's *Musiklexicon* (1916 edition) states that the *Institut français de Florence* is preparing a new edition of all the five-part madrigals, under the editorship of P. M. Masson. Up to the present, however, this has not appeared, nor has anything further been heard of it.

(4) Modern Books Relating to Gesualdo and his Works.

Ambros, Wilhelm, Geschichte der Musik (third edition, 1909, with valuable additions by Hugo Leichtentritt)

Eitner, Robert, Quellenlexicon

Keiner, Ferdinand, Die Madrigale Gesualdos von Venosa (1914)

Kroyer, Theodor, Die Anfänge der Chromatik im Italienischen Madrigale des XVI^ten Jahrhunderts (1902)

Morris, R. O., Contrapuntal Technique in the Sixteenth Century (1922)

Newman, Ernest, A Musical Critic's Holiday (1925)

Prunières, Henri, Monteverdi (Les Maîtres de la Musique) (1924)

Riemann, Hugo, Geschichte der Musiktheorie im IX-XIX Jahrhundert

Vogel, Emil, Bibliothek der gedruckten weltlichen Vokalmusik Italiens (1892)

Winterfeld, Carl von, Johannes Gabrieli und sein Zeitalter (1834)

APPENDIX OF MUSICAL EXAMPLES.

EXAMPLE 1.

EXAMPLE 2.

EXAMPLE 3.

EXAMPLE 4.

EXAMPLE 5.

EXAMPLE 6.

EXAMPLE 7.

EXAMPLE 8.

EXAMPLE 9.

EXAMPLE 10.

EXAMPLE 11.

EXAMPLE 12.

EXAMPLE 13.

EXAMPLE 14.

EXAMPLE 15.

EXAMPLE 16.

EXAMPLE 17.

EXAMPLE 18.